MW01490260

THE

MESSAGES

FROM GOD

2024

CAROLYN DENNIS

FORWARD BY AUDRA KALLIMANIS

1

THE

MESSAGES FROM GOD 2024

CAROLYN DENNIS

FORWARD BY AUDRA KALLIMANIS

DEDICATION

I want to dedicate and thank my family for their love and support.

To my husband, Michael, who is always there for me, is my best confidant and friend. He always has great wisdom and guidance for me. His support and encouragement are unlimited, and I could not walk this journey without him. Thank you, Michael, for letting me take over our time when a video needed to be filmed, and I needed to work with other people's schedules. You are the best and I am so grateful to God for giving you to me as my husband.

To my son Daniel, for being a great encourager and cheering for our YouTube Channel. You are so inspiring with your talent and expertise and truly you are the best son ever.

I love you guys!!!

CONTENTS

THEY ARE GRASPING FOR STRAWS!

MAY 21, 2024 - 57

CALIFORNIA WILL TURN RED!

MAY 22, 2024 - 59

WORLD WAR III?

MAY 23, 2024 - 60

NO MORE BACK-PEDDLNG LIES!

MAY 26, 2024 - 62

45 WILL BE VENDICATED!

MAY 29, 2024 - 64

DAY OF THE VERDICT OF TRUMP!

MAY 30, 2024 - 66

GET READY FOR A ROLLER COASTER RIDE!
JUNE 4, 2024 - 68

TIME FOR PRAYER AND FASTING

JUNE 5, 2024 - 69

BLACK SWAN EVENT

JUNE 7, 2024 - 71

HARRIS TO COLLAPSE IN POLLS & A NIGHTMARE IN THE LIBERAL CAMP

OCTOBER 21, 2024 - 206

HOW DARE KAMALA!

OCTOBER 23, 2024 - 208

WAKE UP MY CHURCH!

OCTOBER 27, 2024 - 210

CHAOS & STRIFE IN THEIR CAMP!!! CELEBRATE! CELEBRATE!

OCTOBER 28, 2024 - 212

GO IN FAITH TODAY! MAKE A DIFFERENCE IN THE LIVES OF PEOPLE!

OCTOBER 31, 2024 - 215

THE PUZZLE YOU HAVE BEEN TRYING TO PUT TOGETHER

NOVEMBER 1, 2024 - 217

A FEARFUL DREAM AND THE MILITARY WILL HAVE TO COME OUT!

NOVEMBER 3, 2024 - 219

15

16

2025 – THE BEST YEAR TO BE ALIVE!

DECEMBER 28, 2024 - 284

**THE MUSIC INDUSTRY WILL CHANGE –
BEYONCE, MADONNA, RHIANNA, TAYLOR &
KATY & OPRAH TOO!**

DECEMBER 31, 2024 - 289

FORWARD

In the midst of a global crisis, when the world seemed to be unraveling at the seams, two girls who love Jesus—Carolyn and Audra—took a bold step of faith. Declaring Your Destiny was born during the uncertain times of the COVID-19 outbreak, with a mission that went beyond the ordinary. Their aim was clear: to reach the lost, to offer hope in the face of despair, and to provide a beacon of light amid the darkness.

During this journey, Carolyn received the gift of prophecy. Prophecy, in this context, becomes a tool not just for foreseeing the future but for declaring and creating it. The power of prophecy provides a divine insight that guides and shapes our destinies. It is through these prophetic messages that many have found direction, purpose, and a renewed sense of hope.
This book is a collection of prophecies Carolyn received from God. It is her hope that it will bring the reader a sense of peace and reassurance that God is with us, that He loves us, and He will not leave us.

With love,

Audra

PREFACE

In February 2024, I was in my home church up at the front worshiping the Lord Jesus. I was in high praise of our King. During the worship I had a vision of me. I saw myself from the knees down. I was wearing my cute girl combat boots and white jeans. From my feet going backwards, there was a line of fire. The Lord said to me "You are walking out of the fire."

I continued my worship and was in awe and wondered what this meant. We went back to our seats at the end of the worship time. During the service, I heard the Lord speak to me again. He said, "You are going to your destiny." Now, I am really in awe and wonder as I have had two very powerful, personal encounters with the Lord in about 30 minutes.

When I got my composure, I wrote it all on a check receipt. I treasure that piece of paper more than you know.

Four years prior, in 2020, Audra and I started an online Bible Study. It was pandemic time and our churches were closed. We live hours apart and we both wanted to fellowship with believers and to study our Bible. The Bible Study went into meeting with people to just recording the Bible Study and posting online. Over the course of four years, day after day, week after week, we had grown our YouTube Channel: Declaring Your

Destiny to 22 subscribers. Yes, 22. Three of them were me, Audra and her husband.

After my encounters with the Lord in February 2024, I was invited to a Donna Rigny Conference at a local church in my area. I went for two days, and it was glorious. Donna taught us about opening ports, the Glory and we had high praise and worship.

The week leading up to the conference I asked the Lord to give a word to Donna for me. I met Donna and she was so beautiful, personable and a wonderful speaker. She truly exemplifies Jesus! But no word from the Lord through Donna to me.

The last session Donna taught us was how to hear from the Heavenly Father. She taught us to praise Jesus and exalt Him for a while. Then tell the Father you would like to hear from Him. You can even ask Him a question. Have your pen and paper and be still and know God. At the time, I did not know, but God was giving me His message through Donna to me.

I was so excited to learn how Donna hears from the Father that I could hardly wait for my family to go to bed so that I could do exactly what she taught us. I went into high worship of Jesus for a period of time and after a while I told the Father that I was listening.

Then I got still and waited with my pen and paper ready. While I waited, I had my eyes closed and visualized Jesus. Then I started hearing in my spirit, three words. I thought, "is it you, Father? So, I started writing and the first message from God started flowing.

This book is a collection of the Messages From God that I have received since March 2024 and the rest of 2024.

God wants to speak to you. Look and listen for Him to speak to you today and every day.

With love,

Carolyn

PS. Any grammatical, misspelling, or incorrect sentencing are my fault. I have strived in my heart to bring you what I heard from the Heavenly Father. Final thought, keep in mind – God is talking to me. This is a conversation, and it might not be grammatically perfect. He speaks to me like I speak.

THERE IS NO ONE LIKE MY SON!

MARCH 29, 2024

There is none like My Son! He is King of Kings and Lord of all Lords. There is no one like Him; nor will there ever be.

Exalt My Son! Give Him the praise, honor, and glory He deserves! He paid the price for all to be free from sin, death, sickness, disease, lack, poverty and more.

He is the Most Precious Gift the world has ever received. He deserves all the praise. Spend time with Him and Me. Give Him an opportunity to be Lord of your life. He will change you from the inside and give you a life filled with love, peace and joy and so much more. He paid the price at Calvary and all you must do is receive Him. Time is short. You know not the time or day that you will meet Your Maker. Receive My Son before it is too late. We have a place for you in heaven. We have planned for you, My beloved children. Keep the faith! Things are going to change quickly, and you will see My Glory. The Glory of your beautiful Savior. Rest in My Glory. Praise in My Glory, rejoice in My Glory, dance in My Glory. I have great plans for you, My children. You shall see and taste My goodness in the land of the living.

~Amen

THE ENEMY WILL FAIL

MARCH 31, 2024

Bless, the Lord, O my soul! Bless His Holy Name! You are high and lifted up. There is none like My Son Who made the ultimate sacrifice for all mankind. Exalt Him and give Him praise! Jesus deserves all the praise. He has paid the price for you to be a part of My Kingdom and to have eternal life in heaven. Jesus is Lord of Lords and King of Kings. He is worthy to be praised.

Watch your motives, your mouth and your actions. People are highly offended in this day. Be mindful to walk in love, truth and justice. You will see justice in this land, Ole' United States. Return to Me, My children, and wait and see.

Things are going to change real soon now and My little lambs will be safe in My care. The enemy is going to take a blow that will hinder them in completing their task. They will not be successful in their attempts to destroy this country and all of you.

I am changing everything. Be expectant! And you will see My goodness. Your enemies will soon be gone, and no one will take My United States.

The time is near. Watch and see My goodness, My Glory poured out of all flesh. Receive My Glory and revel in it. Life will be different now. From the four corners of the earth, I will pour out My Glory that all will see that I

Am the Most High God. It is My earth! I will have the final say!

Your enemies are defeated. Taste the sweetness of the great victory that is on the horizon. Watch My beautiful eclipse. Stand for what is right and turn away from any evil in your life. Keep My Son first. You are loved with an everlasting love. Nothing can separate My children from Me and My Son. You are redeemed from the curse of the law. You are free! Free indeed! Stop your worry and rest in this promise. I am taking care of it all. Stay focused on My Precious Son, Jesus. You will see My Glory, great peace and great victories. You are loved with an everlasting love.

Amen

CHAINS ARE BEING BROKEN!

APRIL 1, 2024

Chains are being broken! Wait and see. Be patient as you wait on Me! My promises are true, and My Son has paid the price. I am answering all of your prayers, and I have great plans for each of you.

The time is at hand, and you will see My Glory manifest on this earth. There will be great miracles, signs, and wonders throughout the earth. There has never been a time like what is getting ready to happen now.

Believe and expect and you will see and taste My Glory. All will not receive it. Pay attention to Me and My Son. Keep your eyes on Jesus! I am not finished taking care of you and getting rid of enemies. They will be gone shortly.

Things take time and I Am the Great God Jehovah, and I have got this in control. I can pour out My Glory and destroy your enemies at the same time. Sit back, relax and rest in Me and My Son, Jesus. The best days of your life are upon you, My dear little children.

Amen

A RED TIDE IS COMING!

APRIL 5, 2024

Holy, Holy, Holy! Holy is the Precious Lamb of God. He is high and lifted up. There is no one like Him. Exalt My Son and praise His Holy Name! The Name above all names! Jesus! King of King and Lord of Lords!

Remember My Son in all that you do. Tell your people about My Son. Do not be ashamed of Him and I will not be ashamed of you.

Stand fast in these days. These are My days, and they will be days of Glory! You have not even begun to experience the goodness of glory that I Am going to our out on the earth!

These are going to be days of awe and wonder. The most beautiful time in the life of you, My precious children.

There will be troubles in the land, but they will be for naught, and I will deal with them as they arise in a speedily manner.

The time is at hand, and you will see and taste My Glory. You are going to be amazed; in awe and wonder at how I deal with your enemies. They are My enemies, too! And time is up. I have given them time and warnings. You say warnings? My Holy Spirit stirred in them to change paths and come to Me. Many have relented and time has run out.

Watch and see. They will soon be gone, and they will never be your problem again in this time. I will deal with them.

I Am the Great God Jehovah. There is none like Me nor will there ever be. I can do signs and wonders in this earth like no other.

I have great plans for each of you, My little children. Plans to prosper you and to give you a hope. Plans of peace and prosperity. A life you never thought possible but only in a dream.

Do not fear the few coming days. I have everything under control and your enemies are already defeated. They will not continue to rule and reign in my beautiful United States.

The earth is mine and the fulness thereof. No man can take away what I have created. Pray for your enemies. And learn to love those who despitefully use you.

The hunter will again become the hunted, and all hell will break out in the enemy's camp. Chaos, confusion, backbiting, treason and turning against one another.

Spend time with Me and My Precious Son. Look to us when you need help and call on the Magnificent Holy

Spirit and He will lead, guide and give you the words of knowledge and wisdom. The direction that you need.

Do not turn to the left or to the right. Avoid the crooked paths and stay on the straight and narrow. Do not be deceived. There will be mockers and those who try to confuse or criticize you.

Keep your eyes on Me and My Son and all will be well with you and your household.

There will be a red tide in this land and the misery and chaos will recede like a gentle ocean tide.

This red tide will restore My precious United States to the land of the free and the home of the brave. A land flowing with milk and honey. A land where children are safe and evil is not allowed or tolerated.

My Bible will be restored, and prayer will return. My young people will gather and sing and dance as they praise My Precious Son.

Rejoice O' United States. You are still the leader I destined you to be. Wait and see! The time is at hand, and I Am coming. Join Me and My Son. Rejoice! Your redemption draw neigh. It is time now and all will be well in the land of the free and the home of the brave.

Holy is the Word of the Lord.

STAND UP UNITED STATES!

APRIL 7, 2024

You are fearfully and wonderfully made. I created the heavens and the earth. There is none like Me! Holy, Holy, Holy is the Lamb of God – Who was and is and is to come.

Stand up United States and believe in Me. Believe in My Power, believe in My wonders, believe in My Glory. Believe in My Son. Receive My Son and learn from Him. Exalt His Name! The Name above all names! Jesus! King of Kings and Lord of Lords.

Holy is the Lamb of God! He is high and lifted up and worthy to be praised.

Tell everyone about My beautiful precious Son. Time is running out and I want no one to perish; not even your and Mine enemies. I love all of My children even those who have turned against Me. I love all with an everlasting love. Choose wisely whom you will serve. Turn away from all evil and look to the glorious light. The light of My Precious Son, Jesus. Magnify His Name and expect that I Am going to move in a mighty way in this earth. We have allowed the evil ones plenty of time to turn from their wicked ways and yet many have only increased in their evil against you and me. It is enough! I Am turning the tide red. It will be red across the land and will say that only God could have done this. Wait and see! Hold on! My great United Stated will flourish and prosper once again. It will even be better than ever before. There will be prosperity and plenty in the land and new creations, inventions, technologies and much more to enhance the lives of My precious little children.

Take care My precious little children and listen carefully to the instruction of the Holy Spirit. He knows everything and He can lead, guide, direct your life in better ways than you ever dreamed. He has the wisdom, knowledge, and creativity. He can help you in the simplest task such as what to wear or the most complex task. Ever things beyond your thinking.

We love you with an ever-lasting heart. We will never leave nor forsake you, Our precious little children. We are three in one. Father, Son and Holy Spirit and we are in agreement and will be with you always. Take time to spend privately with us. We want to have the pleasure of your company. Invite us into all areas of your life. We only come where we are welcome. We have great plans for you and your family. Let us lead and guide you. Allow us to make your decisions and order your steps and direct your pathways. You will have the life we designed, and it will be better than the crooked path of man.

Study My Word and learn of Me. Study My Word and meet My Son in a new way. He is the Way, the Truth, and the Life. There is no one like My Son. Bend the knee and give Him praise, honor and glory. Spread the news about My Son Jesus and all that He has done for you.

Keep My Commandments and love one another with a pure heart. Be quick to forgive even those you feel are unforgiveable. If I can forgive, then surely you can.

Find time for Me today and enjoy your life. Look for My goodness and enjoy your friends and family. I love you with an everlasting heart.

Holy is the Word of the Lord.

THE ENEMIES WILL SOON BE GONE!

APRIL 10, 2024

It is time for My Glory to be poured out on the whole earth. You will see miraculous things that only I can do. There is no other like Me. The earth is mine and it is time for My people to experience My goodness and My glory.

You will see miracle after miracle and the Democratic Party is going to fall apart. Soon they will be no more. Expect great moves on My behalf. It is My great pleasure to do signs, miracles and wonders in this earth. Watch for My signs. Look for signs of My Son. He is coming, but it is not time yet.

You have asked for signs of when things are going to happen. I am giving them to you. Look up! My Greater Glory is coming to this earth. This will be a mighty move and it will break out and it will destroy your enemies.

Rejoice! Rejoice! Rejoice! Great days are upon you. Look to Passover as another marker. What I am doing in the earth will be soon breaking out. Miracles will be commonplace. Peace will reign in My United States and My Beloved Israel.

People will unite in one faith of My Precious Son, Jesus. We are going to have a great celebration. We are preparing a place for you in heaven, but don't plan on leaving for a while. You are not going to want to leave.

My Glory is coming, and your life is going to be so glorious and beautiful. When the days of glory fill the earth, remember Me, MY child and all that I have done in your life. Everything is changing for the good very quickly.

The Days of Glory are upon us! Rejoice, dance, sing, pray and don't forget to eat cake as My Glory is poured out on this earth. Bask in this Glory and the fulness thereof.

Take time to know Me and My Son. It's all about relationship and that is what we want from you. Read My book, the Holy Bible and give your life to Christ, if you have not already.

Count the days and wait and see it is not quickly that I don't change everything. It will change. I can change everything in one day and I am going to do just that!

Holy is the Word of the Lord!

A DAY OF AWE AND WONDER

APRIL 30, 2024

This is going to be a day of awe and wonder. You are going to be so excited and filled with peace and satisfaction. The day is at hand & is here.

It is the day that I change everything. Everything for good. Everything for the Glory of My Dear Son. Everything for My Precious Children.

I have great plans for each of you. Plans for good and to prosper you and to give you a hope. Oh yes, there will still be evil in the world. The enemy will continue to wreak havoc, but My Glory is going to fill the earth and the enemy will be held back from My children. The Glory will push the enemy away. I AM destroying all of his evil plans against you and your family. My children will live long lives of peace and satisfaction.

Stay with Me. Walk with Me and My Son. Love one another. Believe Us. And you will experience the most glorious time in history. My people are calling out for the glory. You call on Me for the Glory. It is coming and your prayers and conversation with Me moves My heart.

Spend time with Me and My Son Jesus. We love you with an ever-lasting heart and we are excited for what is on the horizon.

You are going to be amazed at how quickly the evil ones are "and suddenly" gone.

Pray for them. We love them as We love you and We do not want them to perish either. But it is their choice.

I freely gave mankind freedom to make your own choices. That is My System.

Your globalists want to remove your freedom from you and the freedom to choose.

It will NOT be! You are Mine and bought with the price of My Precious Son

Jesus. They will not steal from you or from Me. The lines have been crossed and now they will know that I AM the great I AM.

I have the final say.

Holy Is the Word of the Lord!

COLUMBIA WILL PAY A STEEP PRICE

MAY 2, 2024

This is a time of reckoning. A reckoning of good and evil. The lines have been sharply drawn and soon there will be no turning back for some.

Harken to My Voice, My little children. Do not compromise your life for fame, convivence, power or wealth. Stand firm as to who you are and to Whom you belong.

You were purchased with the Precious Blood of My Dear Son Yeshua and He is worth the petty problems and the major issues that you are walking through today.

Columbia will pay a steep price for bowing to this tyranny and lawlessness. Lawlessness will be here for a while. But it will be short-lived as My Greater Glory fills the earth.

The rioters and the funders will soon see and know that I AM the Great I AM and Israel is the apple of My Eye.

Repent, I say repent! The time is at hand, and We want all to experience the fullness of Our Glory and not suffer a horrible forever fate.

Choose wisely whom you will serve. Many roads lead to destruction, but My Way is straight and narrow and will protect you and your family.

Watch out how fast I turn the tables of the enemy who has worked furiously to stop, kill, assassinate and bankrupt My anointed son, Donald J. Trump. He is anointed and the time is at hand for you to see and know all that he, Donald

Trump has been doing on your behalf to set you all free. He is working for Me and he and many around him have plans in operation that are not visible yet. Wait and see; he was called, and he took his assignment because he belongs to Me and he loves this country – the great United States.

Oh! The United States will again soon be the #1 world leader that the world loves and respects.

Fear not My little children. I have all in control and the players are all in place. My plan is in full operation, and you will very soon see and experience a new day that will amaze you. You will see the evil ones in handcuffs, tried and given their quick and severe punishment. Pray for their souls as some will repent and see they wasted their precious life serving the enemy – not Me.

I AM merciful and forgive all who repent and those who do repent will be forgiven.

Be quick to forgive as I forgive. Learn to walk in love. Judge not and be merciful and kind to others. I AM love and I love you and all of My children with an everlasting heart.

Soros and company will exit stage left and so will the rest of those global organizations created to enslave, bind and terminate My Creation.

Hold the line and you will see. Walk by faith and keep your thoughts on the victories and not on the minor defeats. All things work for good for those who love Him and We are working all things for good for you and your family.

Pray for the enemy. It might be a hard task, but they need your prayers. Many have been recruited and lured by fame, fortune and sex. Some want out and do not know where to turn or how to get out. Pray for them to know the truth and the truth will set them free.

All will be well very soon. The summer is coming, and things will be hot, but My heat on the enemy will be greater.

Take time for Us today and every day. We know the way you should go and we will guide and lead you on the path we have planned for you. Great is My Precious Son and He is greatly to be praised.

Holy is the Word of the Lord.

~Amen

THE DONALD HAS MY PLAN

MAY 3, 2024

There is no one like Me and My Son Jesus. You can look high and low and try it all and you will only find the life you have desired and dreamed of in Us. We are

Three: Father, Son and Holy Spirit. Three in One. The Trinity. We are here for you always and will never leave you nor forsake you. Your name is written on the palm of My Hand and I know the number of hairs on your head. You are My divine creation and you are loved with an everlasting heart.

Come closer to Me and let Me love on you more. Open your heart to My Precious Son, Yeshua. He is the Way, the Truth and the Life.

I am Love! And Love never fails. My love for you will never fail. You may not understand why I allow some things to happen in your life and why it seems I don't always answer all of your prayers. I work all things for good for those who love Me. I must allow things to happen for My Plan to be orchestrated.

Some of the things that happen filter you and prune you so that you will grow and be prepared for when I can make something wonderful happen. You are always on My

Mind and the Precious Holy Spirit is always with you. He came on Pentecost which is rapidly approaching. Seek Him out and let Him show you the way in all of your daily affairs. He is the orchestrator of your life, and we love you so.

Times are moving rapidly and soon it will be clear why We have allowed the enemy to seemingly have their way. But fear not! As We have everything under control and We had to allow this terrible evil to annulate them for the Greater Glory and the final harvest of souls. Revivals are springing out and soon they will be common talk among many. People will come from far and wide wherever My Glory is. Yes, they will come to soak in My Glory and they will not want to leave. But they will leave and take My Glory with them. Remember Moses after being with Me on the mountain, He had My Glory and wore a veil because the people were in fear of Me. Fear Not! The best days are yet to come. You will see and know of them all and what they have done. How they have lied, cheated and even had people murdered for their fortune, fame and power. It is a great web of all they have done and much of it is connected. I AM untangling the web and going for all of the black widows. I AM the exterminator, and I will have the final say.

My Word is true and there will be truth, justice and righteousness restored in My United States and the world. My plans are working and soon you will see.

My Donald put much into play in the first term and he has the plans that I put in his heart. Do not be afraid of the arrow by night or by the terror of day. Much is a smokescreen and being played out to put fear in the hearts of My children.

Give Us your time and let Us speak to you and answer all of your questions. We can make the hard simple for you in your life. Trust Us as we will always take care of you.

Rejoice, I say rejoice! Have your cake ready to celebrate as you will very soon. I have waited for this time and soon you will understand why it has taken so long and why.

Holy is the Word of the Lord!

THREE DAYS OF DARKNESS

MAY 4, 2024

Three days of darkness. What does this mean? Three days of darkness I will bring on this earth, but not how you think. The darkness will come to light as a new day dawns. Darkness fades when the light comes on. When My Glory fills this earth the darkness will fade.

Yes, but you ask about three days of darkness. Your enemies will manipulate things and there will be darkness in various places, but I AM not bringing darkness but light. I sent them a Light and now this Light will shine brighter as My Glory fills this earth. My children will be dancing and singing, rejoicing, and praising as My Glory touches them and their family.

Put on your Praise garments. Praise moves My Heart. Give My Son Jesus the praise He deserves. He is worthy to be praised. Exalt Him! Praise Him throughout your day and seek His Presence. Jesus is the brother that will never leave you. He is Your High Priest and He is King of My Kingdom. I AM so proud of My Son just as you are proud of your children. I AM a Father, too, and I know how you feel.

You must not be too concerned or focus on what is happening everywhere and when things will happen.

43

Focus on today. Fix your thoughts on what is true, lovely, noble, praiseworthy and of a good report. Think on these things as I told you in My Book, The Holy Bible. Let Me be concerned which I AM concerned. I have all in control. I AM not surprised at what the evil ones have done nor am I worried. When I speak, it is done.

So fear not My little children as all is well. There will be darkness in some places, but it will be short-lived as will all the plans of the deceitful, lying, loser enemy.

Your glorious days are upon you and I sent My prophets to tell My heart, to give you hope and to give you peace.

I love you with an everlasting heart.

Holy is the Word of the Lord

Amen

GOD HAS A PLAN A & B FOR YOU

MAY 5, 2024

Soon you will see new things that I will do for you. Things that you have dreamed of but thought oh, not me. I could never do that or have that because of this or that in your life. Forget all that. I tell you because I love you so. Soon you will see that I AM doing new and beautiful things in your life.

Many will be promoted, be moved, retire, start businesses, get married and have families. You say these are the normal things of life. But each of these will be unusual for the ones that I give it to. People who have no jobs will be promoted; committed homosexuals will see the Light, get set free and marry as they should. I can go the list, but you get the picture.

I AM doing new things in the earth and creating new hearts in My people. I AM making changes like never before and you will love where I am going to take you. Some will travel and some will change locations, but you will see that the best is yet to come.

When I offer the changes in your life, you are free to choose. We gave you free will. Choose wisely as I always have a Plan B. But Plan A is the best. Do not fear the logistics of what I bring your way and whether it will be for your family etc. Trust Me and I will take care of the people in your life, the money and everything else.

Sow seed. Sow it today. Do not delay. Put your seed in fertile ground as I AM getting ready to pour out a harvest of financial release like never before. Sow into My Kingdom. Choose wisely where you sow as all is not good ground. Ask the Holy Spirit where and when to sow and He will lead you and guide you.

Be prepared for the end of the charade is now. Watch and be amazed, at how quickly I expediate justice in this land United States and throughout all of the world. They can run, but they cannot hide from Me. I AM the Great I AM. Be careful who you trust in this time. Many will come in sheep's clothing to kill, steal and destroy your life and that of your loved ones.

I think you know who it will come down, but it will be different than what you think or know. I have a better operation and My operation includes revival, salvation, the Glory and Heavenly Hosts moving in this earth at a greater and mightier pace in history.

You want Me to move, but you just are not seeing My movement. Be still, call on Me. Spend time with Me in your stillness and I will tell you things. Things you do not know. Mysteries to all. Stay with Me and I will show you how to handle the people in your life and how to deal with that pesky problem you have asked Me to fix.

Stay with Me and be still. Ask Me the questions that you want to know. I will tell you the answer and much, much more. I have desired to give you some of My time, but I want you to want to be with Me and for you to start the conversation. Then be still and know Me and give Me time to talk with you. My words are true and there is much for Me to tell you. Ask Me the hard questions but be prepared as My Ways are not man's ways and you may not get the answer you want.

GOD SAYS ENOUGH!

MAY 8, 2024

It is time for the truth to hit the walls of evil. Evil will be destroyed in the land to make way for the Glory invading My earth. The Glory will push out the darkness and the enemy does not see it coming. They are blinded, confused and very confident in their demonic plans to destroy you and all of My precious children.

I will have My Way in this earth. The earth is Mine and the fulness thereof says the Lord of Hosts.

We are at a pivotal point in history. The wheat and the tares are going to be separated and cast into the fiery furnace. Pray for the evil ones that they will repent and escape their horrible forever fate.

I AM Elohim – the Most High God. There is no other – nor will there ever be.

Noah Harari and all of the crew think they can recreate My Creation and steal your mind and your life. It will not be. He has gone too far and must repent before his last day on this earth. He knows I AM the Most High and he has taunted and spit in My face with his evil plan to destroy My people. I am stopping him and his minions. They shall not win. I WIN! And the enemy will remain the forever loser.

48

Tell Me more of what you dream of. I have great plans for you and your house, My little children. And I AM setting you free. But we are free, you say. No, you are not free. You are under man's system that is man-made. Man-made devised to control your movements, your spending, your freedom and your choices. To keep you away from Me. Oh yes, they have plans to take you away from Me. Plans to destroy My Church, the Ecclesia; but, My beautiful Bride of My Son, Yeshua will not be defeated. They will not stop My Church or the movement that I AM sending.

My Glory will fill this earth, and all will know. My Church, the Bride of Christ, will finally be the beautiful, glorious Bride I have created Her to be. A Bride worthy of Jesus and worthy to be called Home. But it is not yet time for the Church to come Home. It is very soon, but We have work to do on this earth first. You are feeling your assignments. Some are on a large, global scale and others in-between, but most are assignments for your family and community.

Love your neighbor as yourself. This means the people around you and all you encounter as you go through your day-to-day life. Love without ceasing. Through love, hearts will be changed and I will trust you more. Love even when it is hard, and they are the unlovable. I love those that hate Me and My Son, Jesus. Love all no matter what. Then I can trust you and promote you for greater assignments for the Kingdom of My Dear Son. Love never fails. Your love will never fail even if it looks like it's not working.

Things take time and your love will not fail with your friends and family and all you encounter. Love all.

I have had enough of the destruction, the fake news, the protestors pretending to be a part of the universities and all of the lies and deception. Enough I say! I will end it all soon and you will taste the sweet aroma of peace in the land and among all people.

Bill Clinton, you are found wanting in the balance. You have been given it all, but you have lied and sold out the country with the help and leadership of your wife. Repent, I say repent. People have died and you know why. You turned your head and ignored the crimes and acted as if nothing ever happened. You are as guilty as she. Repent. Your time is at hand you <u>will</u> meet Me. The money you have stolen to line your pockets will be of no good to you when We come face-to-face. I say repent. The gig is up and many already know. You were taught right from wrong, but you drank the power Kool-Aid, the fame Kool-Aid and the unlimited sex Kool-Aid. Repent, I say repent.

My Son is on go to take you away as He wants His Bride to be with Him in our Home. Not much longer and it will be time for that trumpet to blast and meet Him in the sky. But not yet, My little ones as We have work to do: A great soul harvest and a wealth transfer, too. The Glory is coming. Wait and see. It is almost Pentecost – a landmark day. We have waited for this time and heaven is busy as We are making preparations for the final harvest. So, stay tuned little one and it won't be long.

50

My Donald will return and there will be peace in the land. Oh, there will be problems as the evil one will not give up but know he is out of time on this planet Earth. So, sit back and relax. Spend time with Me. Enjoy each day and rest and play. Make time for your people and don't fret or worry. The time is at hand for My Glory!

Holy is the Word of the Lord!

Amen!

I AM SPEAKING THROUGH MY PROPHETS

MAY 17, 2024

You may not understand everything that I have going on or that I AM doing. Soon you will see, know and understand. The time is here! Get out your cake and plan to celebrate! Be joyful and full of laughter. Sing praise and dance before Me. You are going to be in awe and wonder of what I AM doing and how it goes down.

You know of how I brought the Hebrew children out after 10 plagues. It was not an overnight operation. Neither is this operation now. This is centuries of problems that have been devised long ago. Each generation has spent time recruiting and grooming the next group to further their cause. This evil has manifested over time and now it has come as high as I will let it.

Remember all of the prophecies regarding Israel being restored as a nation. I did that in one day and many did not see it coming. Another time I foiled the enemy.

He does not stand a chance against Me as I AM the great I AM. The Bible is full of prophecies regarding this time, and I have always had My Prophets when I wanted to speak through man. I have raised up men and women to speak My Words for such a time as this. The world has gone rogue and My Voice needs to be heard louder and more clearly during this time. My Voice, the Prophets are giving you pieces of the puzzle, but I have not given all to anyone. I have pieces of this puzzle in heaven with Me.

My Angel Armies are moving and working at a greater speed and might than ever before. They have defeated so much on behalf of My precious little children.

Listen to My Prophets but don't exalt any of them. They are all My Children with problems, people and things that they are doing on My behalf.

When you don't understand or think something is not right, come to Me and talk to Me about it. I want to talk with you, too. My voice is not limited to just My Prophets. Be still and know Me, saith the Lord of Hosts.

I AM your Father and My Words are true. I have vowed in My Book, the Holy Bible to always take care of you. I AM not a man that should lie. I cannot and will not. I sent My Prophets as I sent Moses, Daniel and the rest. Many did not want their messages, and many do not want it now. Their message is from Me to give you hope, truth, and peace.

Be hopeful, expectant and excited. Do not get into strife or argue with those that cannot see. Choose your words wisely and just believe. I tell you again. It is all coming to an end and this will be the most wonderful time in your life. Stay close to Us now as the enemy will roar but the Lion of Judah defeated him then and willdefeat him again. The time is now. Just be patient and see.

53

We love you with an everlasting heart.

Amen

SHIFTY PEOPLE WILL BE REMOVED

MAY 21, 2024

This is the day the Lord has made, and we shall rejoice and be glad in it. All things will be like new as My Glory fills this earth. Problems of old will fade away and vanish. Things will be restored and people reunited. Restoration will occur quickly – I AM the Restorer of the Breach.

Look for My Glory and speak it out. Ask Me to pour it out on you and your house. Hold on. There will still be evil all around, but it will be held back. Darkness cannot be in the light. Darkness always goes away when you turn on a light.

I told you Iran would pay for attacking My Israel. Their leader went down and was killed in the helicopter. There is much more to come against those who have turned on My Israel – the apple of My eye. Fear Not!

The goats and the lambs have been clearly divided. Don't be a goat – come to Me and be My precious little lamb. Meet My Son Jesus and let Us change your life. You will never be the same when you receive My Son as your Lord and Savior.

The United States will have a shift as shifty people get removed, transferred out, demoted, fired or excommunicated. Impeachments will begin in Congress as indictments begin to be brought. There will be many. More than you think, who will be charged, terminated, convicted and sentenced. Some will be put at Guantanamo Bay – others in Federal Facilities. Sentences will be harsh, but right for the crimes they have committed against My people throughout the land of the U.S. Other countries will have trial courts against evil leaders.

Take charge of your households and clean them out. Get out any pagan idols or evil things. Look around and look closely. Something simple from a trip that you took or a sweet gift from a friend could have an evil spirit attached to it. Crush it, get rid of it and cleanse your home and family with the blood of My Precious Son Jesus. Some of your problems will leave when you cleanse your home.

Your problems are not too big for Me. I can handle it and already know about it. Fear Not! I will help you. Call on Me and ask Me what to do. My Ways are not man's ways and I have all of the answers.

Silver and gold are the way to invest. This is My money – not the dollar. Markets will change and you will see a rise in the silver and gold but fear not. I will take care of you even if you don't have any. Remember My Word says – the silver and the gold are Mine and the cattle on a thousand hills. I AM the Great I AM and I always take care of My children.

Spend time with Us today and every day. We will give you direction, answers, wisdom and joy and peace and much more.

We love you with an everlasting heart.

THEY ARE GRASPING FOR STRAWS!

MAY 21, 2024

You will soon see things coming to pass. Iran is a start and you will see great change. Change for good. My children are crying out to Me in Iran and I hear them. They will be free. This is the start of what I AM doing in the Middle East.

The United States is beginning their cleansing. You may not see it happening yet, but soon you will. There will be great change in My land – the land of the free and the home of the brave. The evil regime is on its way down and they will not have anything to redeem them. The evil dance is over. It is time for the indictments and arrests that are coming.

45 will begin the process and his new administration will ensure that all is legal, just and right. Much is in place to begin on day one.

The summer soliste will come and things will heat up, but My plan is in place and they are in great fear and chaos. They are grasping at straws and are pulling out the stops. Do not be afraid. This is all they have left. Surprise there will be in the enemy's amp when they cannot pull off this one last stand. They are fairly sure that this one will work, but they have not counted on Me. The Great I AM. I have not forgotten you My other nations so dear. The plans are in place for your freedom as well. I AM not just focused on the US of A. My eyes roam to and fro over My whole earth. You all matter to Me no matter where you are. I have plans for each one. You are important and vital to Me and My Son. We are working to free you and soon it will be done. You will wake up to a brand-new day and hear the good news of your freedom in one day. Stay tuned and sit tight. Be still and know Me. I have never forsaken or forgotten you.

CALIFORNIA WILL TURN RED!

MAY 22, 2024

The winds of change are upon you, O United States. Look to the east and the west and you shall see great changes. California will turn red.

The border is a temporary problem. There are plans are in place to fix the border very quickly. The people who have come in through your border will be gathered up, detained and departed. Do not fear this problem. I AM in control, and I AM protecting the United States from a massive attack on your homeland. The migrants will be gone, and the cities will clean up. Peace will be restored in the United States.

Hollywood is going to become deadwood as you know it. I AM revamping the entertainment industry.

WORLD WAR III?

MAY 23, 2024

There will be wars and rumors of wars. Much will happen in the coming days, but the end is not for now. There will be World War III, but not for now. The Middle East will settle down and all will be well. Israel will achieve their victory and Iran will back down. Other Middle Eastern countries will be changing their guards as rulers decrease and new ones arise. This is all My plan.

But you ask about a World War III? Yes, it will come, but not for now, first My Glory shall fill the earth. It is time for the harvest of souls, you shall see. As My Glory comes, masses will be saved, and goodness and love shall reign. We are pouring Our love on this good earth because We love you all and want none to perish.

The borders will be secure at last and true vetted will be allowed in. The ones who came will be rounded up and sent back to places where they belong. It will be a quick mission that will come with hitches as many will hide to avoid their fate.

But the Light of My Glory will bring them out and out they will come like ants on honey. Some will volunteer to leave, and others will hide but My Light of Glory will put them on display.

Spend time with Me now and tell Me your problems. Give your cares to Me and let Me solve them. I have all of the answers and will always help. Because of your freewill that I freely gave, you have the choice whether to ask Me or not.

Please ask as I'm here and can show you the way. We can solve any problem – whether big or small.

The clock is ticking and soon it will chime – the beginning of a new day. The indictments and arrest will start on Day 1 as the power will change in DC from dark to light. The swamp will finally be drained, and you shall see what they have really been hiding from you and they thought of Me. I see all and know and am coming to show My Power and might through those who will do My Will and enforce the law. My son Donald will lead the way. We have given him our plans and he is putting them in place. You will be amazed at what is ready and who will go. Some you say yes and some you think no. All is not as it seems. The curtains are closing on their little charade. Get ready My children it is their final curtain. Pray for them as I love them all.

We love you with an everlasting heart.

NO MORE BACK-PEDDLNG LIES!

MAY 26, 2024

Times are a changing. They must to fulfill My beautiful plans for the people of this good earth. Listen in the coming days for outbursts of truth to be blasted out and telecast right in front of you. Things will be said that should have been said in secret and were not meant to be heard. Many will hear these things, and their back-peddling lies will not destroy or eliminate the truth.

These truths will open windows and doors for more truth that is getting ready to pour out. Things of old and things of new. Hidden secrets will pour out soon and this will lead to arrests that they cannot stop or shelter any longer. Be ready and get excited. As this will start the falling of many and they will not be able to prop up anyone anymore as they are going to be trying to save themselves.

Pray for them. Pray they turn to Me before it is too late. Some will try to take easy ways out- but all roads do not lead to Me. Pray for them as We love them too and do not want them to perish.

I have plans and dreams for you. Plans that are going to be your dreams and desires. You say, I could never be that. I have this and that or I am missing such and such. I AM the Great I AM and I can do all things. Nothing is impossible with Me and it is My good pleasure to give you the desires of your heart. So dream and dream big! Take time to dream and ask Me for that desire that you have always privately longed for. I already know as I know all.

You are My precious child, and I love you so there are soon going to be openings in all seven mountains. I want to promote My children to these high levels. So, dream big and ask Me. And watch Me amaze you.

Moms be on your knees for your children. Tell Me what you want for your child and what you need as a Mom. I know it is hard, but you will reap those rewards by being a faithful Mom to the children I gave you. Be kind to them and pray each day for them. They are Mine and I love them so.

For My Want-to-be Moms, ask Me again for your desire. Pray like Hannah and I gave her a Prophet. I have not forgotten you.

Enjoy your life and each day. Find time for Me, your family and friends. Look around and enjoy My Creation. Look at My sunsets and My beautiful sky.

Remember I love you always.

Amen

45 WILL BE VENDICATED!

MAY 29, 2024

President Trump will be vindicated. It will take a moment or two. No one cares about his past whether right or wrong. He is My anointed one and he will be back as the leader of the United States. His seat will be returned to him on the right day, and all will rejoice as the tyrants start getting put away. Trump is My man, and I have chosen him for the task. I made and created him with what he needs to complete the tasks. Give him respect but don't exalt the man. He is a man like you truly flawed.

There is only one man without sin and that is My Son, Yeshua – the King of all Kings and King of My Kingdom. Give Him the honor and praise as He is due. Love on My Son and Trump does too.

Their case is a shambles and it is all that they have. They have paid off the judges, the lawyers and more. For some they used blackmail to further their cause. They have stooped to the lowest levels to hide their secrets. It all is for naught as they will regret what they have done. I AM coming now with My Glory to change the earth. A new day is dawning and soon you will see – the freedom that you have never known about but I have always had for you. Be My little children and call on Me now. I AM listening and I care as a Mama Bird cares for her chicks.

You think they have gone too far, but not for Me. I AM the Great I AM and this is not impossible for Me to fix. I have been waiting for the last one that will repent to Me. I know all of their hearts and who will choose Me. I'M merciful, kind, goodness and love and will wait for one to choose – I love them so much.

The turning of time is right at hand. It is on top of you, but you don't see it yet. My Words are true, and My prophets have told you. Believe Me now and don't have regret. Be My Remnant and expect a new day. Get your cake and prepare to celebrate.

I have sent you many and if you are listening, you know they all are in one form or fashion giving the same. My Glory is coming, and all will change.

The US will be restored and there will be peace in its streets. It will be a new time where people love one another. Many problems will vanish including some hatred. Hatred of people who are different whether color or race. I love everyone and made you unique. Hatred is evil from the pit of hell- put into man through the enemy's schemes. I AM fixing this when I come on the scene.

So, spend some time in prayer and sing praises to us. We love you so much

DAY OF THE VERDICT OF TRUMP!

MAY 30, 2024

There will not be another day like this in My United States. This is a sad day for your freedom, but I AM on the throne, and I AM making the decisions.

Pray for your President, My Donald. Pray for his strength and his energy and his peace. Pray for his family and his team. This is a very hard road they are on but I called then all for such a time as this.

The verdict will not stand, and Bragg and company will pay. They have gone too far, with lies, and hatred with greed and position. They have played with fire and they will get burned and burned they will be. Prison awaits many and they will regret these days for taking the free rights that I gave to this country. Rights developed by the fathers of old when they sought Me for guidance and set up this country. These rights are yours and not theirs to dictate and take. You will see them in shame when all is revealed. Some took bribes and some were blackmailed but they still made a choice to punish this man.

I call you to Me and it is time to pray. Pray and fast for this land and the freedom you desire. Pray for truth, righteousness and justice. The time is at hand and I need you to step up.

My Donald will be dancing and cheering again – but today's a bad day in this land.

But remember My child, I love you so much. I will not let My country fall or crumble as they desire. This land is Mine and was settled for My Son.

The Republican Convention will be the best ever. Truth will reign and you will meet your new VP. He is Mine and I love him, and he will stand for Me. Support him and love him and unite in dignity.

Tomorrow's a new day and My earth will still spin. They have played their last card and they think they have won. But I hold the deck and am in control. The victory is Mine – Saith the Lord.

Don't be gloomy or down. But rejoice and be at peace. All will be well just wait and see. Not much longer My child as I have promised. The moment is coming and all will be right. Remember I love you, sweet dreams and sleep tight.

GET READY FOR A ROLLER COASTER RIDE!

JUNE 4, 2024

I want to tell people that I love them and am working all things for good for those who love Me. The plans of the enemy will fail. I win, you win, and the USA wins.

The events of the coming days are going to be like none other. Hold on as it might feel like a roller coaster ride, but the ride comes to a stop. And when you get off, you might be a bit dizzy. This is like what you might feel in the coming days.

There will be ups and downs. Expect victory on all fronts and defeat for the enemy. But hold on. The enemy is going to pull something else.

Pray for President Trump. He is strong, but a man with feelings and a family, too.

Expect more exposure at Hunter's trial. Hold on a little longer because I AM coming and all will be well.

TIME FOR PRAYER AND FASTING

JUNE 5, 2024

I have much to tell you, My children. I want all to know that I love them with an everlasting love. There is no greater love than the love I have for you, My children. I gave you My only Son as a gift – My greatest gift. Seek Me and know Me and believe My Words.

Oklahoma and Texas – you are loved, and I AM going to fix the problems at your borders and across your states. The political and racial issues will resolve soon.

Native Americans will be restored and have a new freedom that they have never experienced in this United States. All of My children will be free in the land of the free and the home of the brave.

Take time to study My Word. Read My Love Book to you. Learn it and about the people who lived. Many longed to see the days of Glory that you are going to experience. The Bible tells you of the Glory and be asking Me for it. You will never want to leave it once you experience it.

As My Glory comes, the evil ones will shriek or repent. I want them all to turn to Me, but some will not even though I AM merciful and love.

The enemy has deceived so many, and they are going to suffer fates of death, prison and worse. Pray for them and try not to hate them. Pray for exposure in the days to come. Much is coming out and some will shock and amaze you.

My servant, Peter Navarro stood for truth, and he is being wrongly and unjustly punished. All to stop the man that I have picked as the President of your United States. I am helping Peter and the others.

Pray for the J-6ers. Vengeance is mine saith the Lord and there will be vengeance.

You must remember that I have the final say and I say that I win, Trump wins, the USA wins and freedom is going to be restored. It is coming quicker than you think. It will be a great and glorious day and you will rejoice.

Remember I have plans for you and I need My full Body of Christ to fast and pray. Fast and pray for the USA, fast and pray for Trum, fast and pray for peace and freedom in your land.

Stop counting the days or fretting over delays. It is all in My Plan to expose the evil and destroy the plans of the enemy. Humiliation and sorrow will soon be in

their camp. But the camp will be disturbed as they run for cover when the lights shine on them. It is coming and it will be very soon.

BLACK SWAN EVENT

JUNE 7, 2024

Draw near to Me and I will tell you mysteries and secrets that I want to share. Spend time with Me and My Son. We want to commune with you and take you into deeper water. Remember the one who had the vision of being in ankle deep, then knee deep, then hip deep and then neck deep water. We want you to go deeper with US. We are worth it! And you will be so glad you opened your heart.

Pray for fresh anointings and praise My Precious Son Jesus. Praise opens gates, doors, and My heart.

You asked Me about a Black Swan Event. There will be a turn of events that will come. The enemy is going to try something new and explosive. But fear not. I AM on the throne and their plans will fizzle out and only be minor as they always are.

I call you to prayer now as this is the final lap to restoration of this country. I need all hands-on deck to pray for the USA. The safety of this country. Pray against cell groups on the inside and the swamp monster in your government.

You will hear of events caused by organized terrorist cell groups in your country. They are making the plans and there is time to stop and minimize the attack. Pray and believe. They have come in through the open border with plans in place. There is a massive organization but fear not as I AM on the throne, and I AM greater than their plans or their organization.

Pray! I call you to prayer! Pray against this organization and ask Me for the defeat of this enemy.

Your country is battling two enemies. It is two internal wars. The monster swamp government and the illegal terrorist border invaders. Pray for these groups to turn to Me. I can change their hearts, but they must receive US.

Pray for the plans of the enemies and these organized Mafia to be delayed, destroyed and fall apart. Pray for chaos in their camp. Pray for peace in the USA and throughout the world. Pray for peace. Pray for the Glory to fill My earth. Pray for the peace of President Trump and his family as they await a sentence. All will be well. I work all things for good for those who love Me and My Donald loves Me. I have anointed him for such a time as this.

Speak to the mountains in your life. Use your authority and speak to the mountains men have built in this country. They will crumble and truth, justice and righteousness will be back in the USA.

A WARNING TO HOLLYWOOD!

JUNE 10, 2024

Great and wonderful things are getting ready to happen in My earth. Be expectant and see the splendor and Glory poured out. See the enemy sink down in front of you. See truth, justice and righteousness returned in this land and all over My world.

How can this be you say. I AM the Great I AM. I can do all things. Nothing is impossible with Me. There is much to tell you of what all will happen in the coming days, weeks and years. Much will be reversed that the enemy has done over the past three decades. You thought it was only 3 ½ years. No, My child. These problems started long ago but what I need to fix is recent and soon you will see.

I AM going to fix racism in this country. The problem is not as bad as the media wants you to think. The government, media and Hollywood want you to think that all races hate each other. Not so! There is much love of all of My people to each other. To eliminate the racism, I will start with the Media and the government. Yes, there will still be haters. But I AM going to eliminate the propaganda problem regarding racism. I love all of My children.

Hollywood is going to have a cleansing. So much evil flows through Hollywood. They have taken truth and promoted evil in movies, TV and causes dome of My children to fall. But I redeem all and come to Me. I love you. Just call on Me. I AM merciful and I will restore what they have taken from you. A warning to Hollywood! Stop exploiting My children. Stop using people and throwing them away like trash. Stop persuading people to do things for fame, fortune and money. Hollywood, how many of My precious children have you destroyed?

There will still be entertainment and entertainment that you enjoy. But thanks to the saints in Hollywood and the LA area who have prayed for cleansing for decades. I AM coming and working all things for good for those Who love Me. Celebrities in the evil satanic rituals – turn away and return to Me. I still love you. Fall on your knees, repent and cry out to Me. You are My prodigals, and I AM a good Father and will take you back. Repent or there will be a fate worse than death.

Seek Me early in your day. Talk to Me throughout your day. Spend time with Me before you go to bed. Give Me a few minutes of your time. Tell Me your problems. I have the answers. And I will help you. I know the best situation and how to get there. Remember I love you always and I want you to enjoy your day!

ENOCH HOLDS THE ANSWER!

JUNE 19, 2024

Enoch holds the answer. The Book has the key to what you have been searching and listening for. Decipher the Book of Enoch and you will easily figure out My Plan. Some may know because you have studied; others will find out as they read Enoch and some will still not get this hidden mystery.

Fret not My little ones as I AM in control. All of you, My children, will be protected. The day will happen, and the world will change. All does not depend on an election or on one man. It depends on Me! So, get cake and prepare to celebrate. All will occur in My Book so true. Some have happened and there is more to come. But fear not, My Little Ones. Look at Moses when all were protected but the naysayers against Moses? Look to the Red Sea when I saved My children, and the evil ones died. Read My Book of Exodus. I wrote it too. My Book tells a journey from beginning to end. Ask the Holy Spirit as He knows all. He can give you the answers and give the discernment you need. The puzzle is almost together and it is time.

I AM coming against them. Did you pray for them? Pray they repent before it's too late. Pray for their repentance and turn to My Son. Fear not My children as it is all in My

Plan. Things will change suddenly, and you will rejoice in your land.

Enoch holds the answer. The Book has the key to what you have been searching and listening for. Decipher the Book of Enoch and you will easily figure out My Plan.

Some may know because you have studied; others will find out as they read Enoch and some will still not get this hidden mystery. Fret not My little ones as I AM in control. All of you, My children, will be protected. The day will happen, and the world will change. All does not depend on an election or on one man. It depends on Me! So get cake and prepare to celebrate. All will occur in My Book so true.

HAVE YOU READ THE BOOK OF ENOCH?

JUNE 19, 2024

Take charge of your day and don't delay to tell people of My Precious Son, Jesus. He was slain before the world and rose on the third day. He died that all (men) may have a relationship with Me. He died for one and for all.

Precious are you, My Saints. I love you with an everlasting love. A love that you can only have when you receive My Son, Yeshua as your Lord and Savior of your life. Believe Him now. Do not delay. You know not the hour or the day when your time is up. We will receive you and We will help you and you will have a new life in My Son Yeshua.

Be still today for a bit and know Me. Sit in your garden or your prayer closet or your car and give Us a few minutes of your time. We can handle all of your busyness and make it easier and quicker.

Do not fear the events of the coming days. The media will make it seem worse than it is with their rhetoric language and their sounds and music. Ignore all of that and keep your eyes on Me. I see all and know all and have everything under control. I have told My Prophets much and you have listened. Fear not as the best days of your life are upon you.

Enoch walked with Me and then he was not on the earth anymore. I brought My son Enoch home and he is here with Me. He is My first prophet, and you should study His book. They did not put it in My Love Book, The Holy Bible, to hide the truth of what I AM getting ready to do in this earth. Find the Book of Enoch and read it and you will receive more revelation knowledge of My plan. This is a large piece of the puzzle.

I AM the Father of Abraham, Isaac, and Jacob and I can and will do miracles, signs and wonders in My earth. It is not time yet and I AM going to do something new like no other that I have done before. I AM not a copycat, and I do not plagiarize Myself. This will be a new thing, and it will be marvelous in your eyes. You will be truly amazed and it will make your ears tingle. When this happens, the world will know that I AM the Great I AM. Look at Exodus and the wonders I did there. I eliminated much of the evil in a second and I did it several times. I AM going to do it again in a new way.

I have given you many clues as to the mysteries of this time. Don't wait on a prophet to fill in the blanks. Ask Me yourself. Prophets are people who are imperfect trying to get it all right, but they do not know it all. Trust Me and seek Me. Listen to your prophets, and I want time with you, too.

I love you with an everlasting heart.

THE CLOWN SHOW IS ALMOST OVER!

JUNE 20, 2024

Send out the clowns. The clown show is almost over. The time is up and soon you will see.

You say, how much longer? Things have picked up speed and things are moving at at a more rapid rate. You see the lies. You watch Biden an they say he is fine. How can that be? Unless they are faking. But they are faking, but it is not what you think.

Biden has the real problem as does the actor who stands in for him from time to time. Quite sad. The old guy can't enjoy his last days and have some peace. How tortuous each day for them to get him ready for what he knows not and most of the time. He would rather be at the beach eating his ice cream.

There are times in men's lives that they come to a crossroad and must make a choice which way to go. Choose carefully the path you go down and whom you shall follow. There are many deceivers in the land, and they are looking for whom they can devour. Avoid the scammers, the telemarketers and strangers who randomly call you or approach you on the street. Ask Me before you approach people or give them money. I want you all to be very generous, but I will direct you on what is good soil and what is not. Deceivers are not good soil.

Exalt My Son Jesus and give Him all of the praise. My Love Book is about My Son and a guide for your life. You must read it to understand it. Take a few minutes every day to read My Love Book. My Bible is Alive. It is the Living Word and The Word became Flesh and reading My Book a little everyday will change your life. You say, you want more of Me and My Son?

Seek Us first and the Precious Holy Spirit. Give Us your first fruits of your day and read Our Love Book for a few minutes. Your days will run smoother. We will give you rest and peace and We very much want the pleasure of your company.

Be hospitable as you never know when you are entertaining angels and be friendly to people. Love one another. We first loved you. Return the love to Us and the world.

Amen

A REBUKE FOR THE SAINTS/CHURCH!

JUNE 23, 2024

How can you look at entertainment shows on TV and read gossip magazines and then condemn My Anointed ones who have sinned. You relish on the gossip of celebrities and think their adventurous lives are just part of their lifestyle. And then you dare to judge My servants who have fallen into sin. I AM dealing with My servants. Remember I instructed you to judge not. That means everyone. An then I told you to do no harm to My anointed. Church, I AM calling you out. You need to be praying for your brothers and sisters who have been shepherds who are stepping down due to sin. Judge them not. They are still Mine and I love them with an everlasting heart.

Pray for them and their families. Those who repent and come to Me with a pure heart and they will be restored. You may see restored as one thing and I may see it differently. They will be restored to Me, and I will decide the rest.

THE GREAT ESCAPE

JUNE 24, 2024

You will know it when you see it and you will see it soon! They think they have all in control, the Debate, the NY Judge, and everything else they are maneuvering but they have discounted Me! I AM that I AM! And they cannot stop what I AM getting ready to do in the earth. It is the Great Escape. The escape of My little ones from the great evil that is running My good earth. The evil ones will not escape but are facing fates worse than death. Some are already gone, and you think they are still here. Soon you will see masses gone. Gone like the wind.

Where did they go? This is a mystery. Have you read the Book of Enoch? Enoch holds the key. When you hold the key, you can see what is coming. It will happen in one day. But who can escape the Great and terrible day of the Lord? Only the elect. Fear not My little ones as you have nothing to fear. I promised to take care of you and My Precious Son died for you.

Protection and care are a part of Our covenant. Exalt My Son and give Him the Glory. Great is His faithfulness and He is worthy to be praised.

Now go out today and enjoy the moments. Rest some, dream some and talk to Me about your needs, wants and your desires. I AM a good Father and it is My pleasure to give you the desires of your heart.

A MAJOR GLOBAL EVENT!

JUNE 24, 2024

A major global event is getting ready to occur. It is not what you think. It is not nuclear, and it is not the rapture of the church. This final move will prepare the Church to come home, turn sinners into saints and bring revival on a global scale.

I have pretty much told you, but I am launching a surprise attack on the enemy. I have told you the enemy will soon be gone, and they absolutely will. They have had time to repent and it is time for Me to move.

Stay close to Me in the coming days and do not fear. This move is against the truly evil non-repentant. It is not against the wayward who will return home to Me.

You will not miss this. The world will not miss this, and you will be rejoicing and dancing in the streets. Eat cake and send gifts to one another. Your preparation is prayer, get some cake and pray some more. Walk by faith and enjoy your time with Me and My Son Yeshua. We love you so. Spend time with your family and friends.

The show is ready to start. I love you with an everlasting heart.

THEY WILL BE GONE SOON!

JUNE 29, 2024

You have witnessed some of the embarrassment and humiliation that I AM bringing on the enemy. The debate was a start. Wait and see what happens next. They are scrambling and worried and in great fear. The Bidens will not let go, especially the family. The Dems have run out of choices and their party sees a massive upset in government control after the election. They will be gone soon. All of them and it will be in mass. Hold on. Stay tuned and secure your seatbelt. The party is just getting started.

Watch for My Glory. I have told you as the Glory fills the earth, the evil will fade away. It all is going to happen in one day. I do not need more than one day to accomplish this mission of setting the world free from this monstrous evil.

Do not fear as it all starts happening. Alarms may sound, but I AM on the throne, and I AM protecting my little lambs. Fear Not!

Did you know at the Marriage Supper of the Lamb, there will be beautiful wedding clothes, jewels and even wedding gifts? Heaven is in great preparation for the Marriage Supper of the Lamb. To have a marriage supper, there must be a wedding. We are excited for the Bride of Christ to come Home and to be in preparation for the marriage of the church to My Precious Son Yeshua.

The Glory filling the earth will begin the preparation period for My Saints. When the Glory fills the earth, you will witness sinners saved. People you thought were doomed for hell. When the Glory fills the earth, you will witness miracles, sickness eradicated in masses. Miracles, healings – People waking up healed.

Limbs growing back. You will hear shouting and dancing and praising. When My Glory fills the earth; I AM excited for this time in history, so We want to bestow

Our Glory on our children and We are excited for you to come Home in the not too distant future. But not quite yet. My Word must all be fulfilled for this time and

We are awaiting the billion-soul harvest. It is coming. Be prepared to tell people about Jesus. How you found Him and met Him. Tell people how wonderful your life is with My Son. Tell people how much We love them. Invite them to receive My Son. It is the perfect plan.

Have you prayed today? Spend a few minutes in your prayer closet or convert your car into a prayer mobile. Just give US a few minutes of your time. Sing songs to US. We love your sweet voice. Give Us your heart and let US manage your day. We know all of the answers and the outcomes. We love you and want you to be excited and expectant for the coming days and events in the earth. Enjoy

the day!

Love,

Abba Father

MIRACLES WILL BECOME COMMONPLANCE

JUNE 30, 2024

I AM merciful and I AM a good Father. Soon you will see My goodness poured out on this good earth. They will know My power and the world will experience My greatest move to rid the world of evil and to save My precious children.

Salvation is going to be instantly commonplace when My Glory fills the whole earth. You will not miss it. Many will have to stop what they are doing as the Glory overtakes them. Some will fall out for a short time. This is all to glorify My Precious Son, Jesus. Everything is for Jesus.

The miracles that are going to happen will be commonplace. You will hear and see of many healings, financial problems solved, families reunited, relationships restored, prodigals coming home, addicts set free and people getting set free from proverbial illicit lifestyles – such as LBGQ and others.

I AM eradicating racism. My Glory will pour out love that you cannot deny. And this notion of everyone for themselves and push and shove... honk the horn will minimize. Love will abound in the hearts of My children and love never fails. I AM love and I never fail.

My Glory shall fill the earth until My Son comes to get His beautiful Bride – the Church without wrinkle or blemish. The evil ones cannot stop Me and they are going to deeply regret that they ignored Me and choose the path for greed, fame, fortune and power.

Do not think that everyone left when the Glory comes will choose My Son Jesus. There will still be those who reject Him. We want all to come to US, but We gave mankind freedom of choice, and I AM not a man that would lie. I AM a covenant keeping Father and I abide by My design, rules and commandments. You should too.

What are you doing to spread the Gospel of Jesus? Tell people, start a Bible Study (a home group), start a Social Media group, post memes about My Son. There is much you can do without going on a mission trip to a foreign land. Ask Me and I will direct you as to your mission, a destiny for US. We have great plans for you to prosper and to give you a hope. Let US direct your day and your pathway. Everything will be better.

You have not because you ask not. Dream big and bigger and ask Me for your dreams. It is My good pleasure to give you the desires of your heart an I will not give you something that will harm you are take you away from US. I have the best plans for your life.

That event in your life that is causing you pain – bring it to Me and let Me heal your heart. Whether you were the sinner, or someone sinned against you, I want to bring restoration to you and deliver you from this. Spend time with Me and I will make it a memory that is no longer traumatic or painful but one that I have turned to good because I love you. You are Mine and, on My heart, always. The best is yet to come. We love you with an everlasting heart.

Q, WEATHER EVENTS & YOUR AUTHORITY

JULY 3, 2024

Q is one person, and you know who it is. The Q is legit, and it is highly orchestrated with several players coordinating the components. Q gives the time, the date and the calms precisely. If you have followed Q, you know much of the plan being orchestrated by the good group or the white hats. Pay attention to key words, times and dates. They are very specific and their meaning always points to something.

Q take one than that one and there are two very intelligent writers and authors who handle all of the Q drops. It is part of their plan and My Plan to set up some of the greatest revelation of this time. Q's mask will come off and you will say – I should have known.

The weather events will continue until there is peace in My Israel. The actions of the US against My Israel have greatly affected the weather and the climate in the United States. They call it climate change. Only I change the climate and when the Eagle does not fully support My Israel than I change the climate. When the US steps up and does truly right by My Israel, then the climate will settle down.

The Globalists invented the term climate change to promote their propaganda, increase your spending on things you do not need and to control more of your life. Don't buy into it. I AM the Great I AM and I control all of the weather and the storms.

Do not fear the weather. Use your authority to calm the storms as Jesus did on the Galilee. Use your authority to calm the other storms in your life as well. Learn the authority you have in Jesus and use it against sickness, debt, poverty, lack, strife, fear and depression and anything evil or demonic coming against you and your family.

You can calm the storm, and WE want you to know how to do it. This is a powerful gift My Son gave to you. All authority of Jesus has been bestowed upon you. Learn to use it and get your heavenly language if you don't have it yet. These are powerful tools to fight the good fight of faith.

Now get some rest, Tomorrow is a big day, and you don't want to miss it.

THEY WILL ALL BE GONE!

JULY 8, 2024

You are going to get up one day very soon and they will all be gone. Gone as in gone. People will say where are they? They will hunt for them like they did Elijah (vision of TV announcements). Millions of people are missing from the earth. They will use aliens, blackholes, climate change and the like to consider where they have gone. But in their hearts, they will know that it is I, Elohim, Who has fulfilled My Promises.

My Glory will fill the earth as they depart. Remember My Child there will be many still here that have not met My Son, Jesus and they will be looking for answers. Be ready to give them. A loving and merciful Father has saved us all from the evil that was trying to destroy all of My Goodness in the earth. The enemy, satan, will be disarmed but over time he will regroup, and I will deal with him again. He nor the evil ones can stop what is coming. It will make your ears tingle and it will change everything.

Some will be gone that you did not suspect, and some will remain that have been uncover for Me and you thought they were bad. I know the hearts of all, and it is My choice what is coming and who will be gone from the earth. The earth is Mine and the fullness thereof. Pray they repent before it is too late.

It seems outlandish but I have done this in a different way and on a smaller scale. You will not miss this major event that is closer than you think. The world problems will solve on their own with much of their leadership gone. The United States will return to the country the Founding Fathers dreamed of and made great sacrifice to be here.

Global issues will be gone, and it will be a time of peace and great harvest in the earth. Be preparing for your role as a Disciple of Jesus. You are called to be in the mission field. That could be on your computer, in the grocery store, or something in a public setting. Ask US what your part is. Spread the Gospel for this end-time harvest My children, you are needed and My Son, Jesus gave you the great commission. Step up for Him and for the love of fellow human beings.

For My Servants who have been obedient to be debt-free, I have great rewards for you. Spend some time with Me and let's talk about your future and your dreams. My plans for My Good stewards will be rewarding and fulfilling. Do not fret or be anxious, just wait to be amazed.

THE GLORY, NESARA & BIDEN

JULY 6, 2024

I have great plans for you and your family. Fear not as the days are coming when all of these things that I have foretold are coming to pass. You shall see it all very soon. But for some their hearts will melt and fear will overtake them. For some fear will be their friend as a horrible fate awaits them.

But you, My Precious child have no reason to fear. I AM on the throne, and I AM working all things for good for those who love Me. So, fear not the alarms, the weather, the government and the enemies of Mine. Fear not wars and rumors of war. All will be well with My Precious children.

I have promised My Glory shall fill the earth and I AM a promise keeper. We are excited in heaven to pour out Our Glory upon the earth. Everything is going to change, and it will all be in one day. So, fear not and get your cake and be prepared to celebrate. Because celebrate you win! For many reasons – you have no idea what you have been living under and I AM setting My people free and it is all for the Final Great Harvest before My Precious Son, Yeshua comes for His Bride.

Nesara is from ME, and it is going to happen. This is all a part of MY Plan and to right the money-bondage that has been placed on MY children for centuries.

Watch for the change in your debt. Expect it, believe for it and soon you will see all of your debts wiped out in one day. This is MY Plan, and I show men and women of Mine how to implement what I want in the earth.

Nesara does not mean you will not have to pay for things, or you will not have to work. This reset is to set you free from the financial slavery and bondage that you are in by your government.

Some have already woken up to being debt-free and soon you will as well. Remember I gave man free-will and I work through man. This is a plan devised by ME implemented through men to set you 100% free. Don't doubt and don't fear. But don't go crazy spending money either. Stay where you are, have faith and let ME work MY plan. All will be well. I AM Abba Father, and I take care of MY children.

Did I not tell you the Biden's will go to Delaware soon? Not much longer and they will be a memory. So sad what this family has put this man through for greed, fortune, power and perks. They should repent. But much worse is what this family and those around them have done to MY precious United States. The agendas of the elitists, the Globalists and the Marxists have taken advantage of a man with cognitive issues and a family willing to sacrifice and give anything to have what they have gotten. I AM going to deal with all of them. The Bidens, the puppeteers, the greed mongers and Obama. This is MY problem with all of these people. Pray for them again to repent and turn to ME. Time is up for some! Today's a hot day and go and play. Spend time with the people in your life. Be quick to forgive and turn the other cheek. Remember We love you with an ever-lasting heart!

TRUMP WILL COME BACK STRONGER!

JULY 13, 2024

President Trump will come back stronger and will gain even greater support. This was another failed deep state operation to stop President Trump and more is coming from the deep state. It was organized and orchestrated, but I protected My Donald to have minimal injury.

Pray for President Trump, his family and the men and women that would lay down their lives for him. There have been other attempts, but they have not materialized or made public. It is time to fight the good fight of faith and believe that I AM fixing the problems.

The blow to President Trump will give him more favor in the eyes of those on the fence. The Dems cannot come up with a plan and someone came up with this one. In time, you will learn the truth and the truth will reign throughout the land. Get ready for more and more exposure. This event today will open more doors for the exposure the indictments and the dismantling of the evil deep state.

The RNC will be the best ever with great speakers and news of the man I picked to be your VP. The RNC will be the most watched ever and President Trump will rally and cheer again. I AM the Great I AM. I know their plans before they make them. This was My Hand on My Donald in his life and health being spared. The gunman was an accurate sharpshooter, and you see he did not miss. I protected My Donald and I will use this evil for good for those who love Me.

Your prayers are much needed today and every day. Take time to pray. Pray for the USA pray for a smooth, peaceful RNC, pray for Trump and his family – their health, security, strength, and peace. Pray! My prayer warriors are in the trenches now and you need to execute this powerful tool I have given you. My Son Jesus taught you to pray. I have told you to buckle your seatbelts. Saddle up and fear not. This ride is not over and soon you will see more pandemonium from the Deep State. They are out of options and have no one that will beat Me and My Plans for this country and President Trump.

There is no one like Me and My Son, Jesus. We win and you win. I never said it would be a smooth ride but it will soon be over, and you will be celebrating. Look at the Rally's, look at the signs and flags and bumper stickers. There are more on our side and the Dems know it. We are unstoppable and unbeatable. My Hand is on President Trump and the agenda, he has to restore My beautiful United States, to the land of the free, the home of the brave and a land that truly truth, justice and righteousness and does not act like that through lies. Say your prayers. Get some rest. I AM on the throne, and all is and will be well.

THE WORLD WILL VERY SOON KNOW
MY POWER AND MY MIGHT
JULY 15, 2024

This will be an exciting, turbulent week filled with celebration and events that change the course of history. I protected My Donald, and I will protect him again. The radical left will try other attempts on his life. Remember there are other ways to kill someone besides a gun. But I will protect him and keep him strong. He is working My Plan and soon this terrible tyranny will be gone. Gone as in gone! I have told you this before ans I AM reminding you as WE are rapidly approaching the day when this critical event happens and again – They are gone!

Some things will be the way you think, and others will be quite different, but the end result is there will be freedom in MY land and in MY world. A freedom that only I can give. Man has enslaved you all with taxation, tariffs and more taxation. The taxation is going to change. Remember I told you about Nesara and it is real. The real deal. Don't put your trust in man or just one man. Trust Me, Abba Father and trust My Son Jesus. He is the Way, the Truth and the Life. The world will very soon know My power and My Might. Some will respond to Me and others will attempt to run and hide. But you, My Dear little children I will take care of you and protect you always. Keep your eyes on My Son.

This week you will meet your next VP. Pray for this man and his family. The left will turn up the heat on him starting Thursday night. I will protect him too and all of his loved ones. Trust Trump's pick as this is My Choice for this great nation that I love.

Have you prayed today? We know you have a lot going on and we want you to have a beautiful, fulfilling life. Give US some of your day. Check in with US throughout the day. Pray in all circumstances and love one another and be quick to forgive.

We love you with an everlasting heart and soon you will see one of the greatest moments in history happen right in front of you.

Don't fret or worry and keep your eyes on My Son. A new day is upon you and all will be well.

I love you,

ABBA Father

TRUMP AND VANCE WILL CHANGE THE WORLD

JULY 15 & 17, 2024

July 15 PM - FIRST NIGHT OF REPUBLICAN CONVENTION

Tonight is the start of your country's return to being the powerhouse it was created to be. Trump and Vance will change the world. The wars will stop, no more rumors of war, debt will decrease, living expenses will go down, the border will be secured and the illegals will be expelled. The woke agenda will fade away and prayer will return to our schools. Christian values will be taught, and America will truly be free again.

Pray for Trump and Vance. They are men with homes and families and things in their lives that go on just like in your life. But their problems must be dealt with in private and then they step on the stage. Everyone is not always happy or on board, but the mission to these two men is greater and it is from Me. Know that I have picked them and they will succeed. Your part is to pray and participate where you can. Vote!

Do not let the Dems back peddling change your thinking. They are not truthful and spin things around for their good, not yours or Mine. I AM dealing with them and soon they will be gone. All of them! I have told you before to stay tuned and look for it.

July 17 AM

And the world will soon know that I AM the Great I AM. There is no one like Me. Turn to Me before it is too late. Tell others about ME. We don't want any to perish. We love all. Saved and unsaved.

This great event must happen to rid the evil from the land and to bring in the Great and Final Harvest before My Son comes. Please know this is an act of love for My precious children.

Your cries and changing and they will be filled with joy and peace. Get ready. Be prayerful and Fear Not! The best is yet to come.

THE TIME HAS CHANGED!

JULY 20, 2024

The time has changed. Can you sense the change? Can you feel it? Change is in the air and it is time for great change in My earth. You have seen the Dems falling apart, My Donald's court cases going away and the best political convention ever.

You have seen Me miraculously save Donald Trump from being assassinated and much more. You have met MY VP pick, J.D. Vance and soon you are going to see bigger and greater events happen in MY earth. Do not be troubled or bothered and fear not.

The September Surprise will be a shock and a surprise to many, but it will be the event that will change the course of history. Your life will never be the same and soon the world will know that I AM the Great I AM. Be ready. Be in your prayer closet and do some fasting. Give US some time and love one another.

There is no one like MY Son and MY Son paid the price for all to know ME. For all to have eternal life with US in heaven. Pray for the lost. Call them by name. I AM answering all of your prayers and I have not forgotten that one that you love that is lost. I AM a Way maker, and I know the way to each one's heart. I will make that way and change their life.

Get ready to be amazed as MY Glory fills the earth. The Glory will bring in many lost ones. You will never want to leave MY Glory. Men have wanted to experience what you, MY precious children are going to receive. This is a great time and WE are very excited in heaven as WE are ready for the billion soul harvest and for the Homecoming of the Bride of Christ.

This is going to be a time when you will physically see people falling down and worshipping and repenting of their sins. Some will be in awe and worship and some will be admitting their sins as they recognize ME and MY Son. It is going to happen in the street, in the stores and everywhere when people get a taste of the

Glory, their lives will be forever changed. Some will run and hide and not receive US. But now is the time for the Glory and the Final Soul Harvest. WE are pouring out OUR love on this earth as WE want no one to perish. Fill up your tank and drink the Living Water. Eat the Manna, I have given you: The Living Holy Bible.

Kamala is a problem for the Dems, and she will be around for a while. The problem with Kamala is they know not what to do with her and deals are being made and threats of what to do. Joe will exit and then there is Kamala. She's on the ticket and there she will stay. But soon she will go away. Pray for her and her family. I gave you instructions to pray for those in authority and unrightfully she and Joe are in authority now. Pray for them all. They need your prayers and I want them to repent for all of it.

KAMALA & THE MARGIN

JULY 21, 2024

This is going to be an exciting time filled with drama and lots of laughter. She is laughing and laughing she will do. Listen to her laugh as she thinks she is climbing the ladder again. Her climb will be very short lived. I have told others this would happen and now it is time. Just a short transition in power and then you will be free. She will be forced to pack up and go where she may – not to return to the stage or bother MY USA.

Glory days are upon you and soon you will see the USA restored to the great land of life, liberty and justice. Justice and truth for one and for all. My Way is Truth and truth is speaking out.

They cannot hide their secrets any longer and the truth will pour out. They had to admit Ole' Joe is not competent and soon they will tell you more of their secrets and mysteries. Hold on and sit tight. The show will get better. Fear not and believe and know that I AM in charge. I have all of this in control as MY Plans unfold. They will regret what they have done for their power and fame.

Be patient MY little ones as all is revealed – a piece at the time but now they are big pieces.

Trump and Vance will take this country by storm and get the margin that is needed to have no appeals. The margin will reign and there will be no backbiting or down-slide. The margin will give Trump and Vance what they need to start on Day

1 with making MY Country great again. I gave Trump the Make America Great Again, and I put it on his heart. Remember to pray for Trump and Vance and pray for the margin. The margin it will be.

KAMALA, THE SEPTEMBER SURPRISE AND THE GREAT WEALTH TRANSFER

JULY 22, 2024

Kamala is going to divide the party more and cause more problems than they already had. The sins committed to get here are catching up with her and the Dems and they are on a cause of destruction. Stay tuned and sit tight. The show will get better and better. Fear not for your country. I will protect you from her and what she does or does not do. No evil shall befall you neither shall any plague come neigh your dwelling. All will be well in the land of the free and the home of the brave. MY USA. I love this land and will protect you and keep you against all internal and external threats. No weapon shall prosper which forms against thee.

This day and this time will soon pass, and you will be cheering and celebrating. It is almost over.

Draw near to ME MY little ones and know that I love you. I sent and gave you MY only Son – JESUS – WE love you so and want you to know US more. Take time to talk with US. Take time to listen Be still and know that I AM God.

The September Surprise will be a critical event in history. The enemy is going to be surrounded and surprised on multiple levels. It is MY surprise, and it will entail more exposure and details of how everything is coming together.

September will be a month ending the hot and heated summer. The elections will be in full swing with the Dems losing more and more.

The current Kamala surge is propaganda and a relief that Joe is leaving. Reality will set in and the majority will agree they don't want the current administration's reality. Lay out the pieces of the puzzle and what do you see? Much you did not know three years ago and much you still do not know. The conspiracy theorists will be known as the truth teller. As much truth is leaking out every day. The truth is coming and are you ready for the real truth? The hard truth has what has been happening in MY world. They have enslaved MY people, and I have had enough. You are to be free, and this freedom will be a new life!

The September Surprise will bring joy and delight to the masses, but the Kobal will be hiding. The Kobal's days are numbered and soon they will not have all of the gold or the silver. Silver and gold is mine and the cattle on a 1000 hills. The wealth of the wicked is laid up for the righteous and now it is time. Time for MY children to be free of the enslavement, debt bondage and living paycheck to paycheck. I know the hearts of MY children and who I can trust. The Great Wealth Transferis for MY Children and to fund the Gospel of My Dear Son, Jesus.

Love,

ABBA Father

THE SUPREME COURT, CONSIPIRACY THEORISTS AND ISRAEL

JULY 27, 2024

The Supreme Court will change the course of history with their decision in the 2020 election. It is coming very soon, and it will change everything. There will be unrest, chaos, confusion and what-to-do moments. But trust ME now as this critical event changes history, indicts criminals and opens a floodgate of issues, policies, apologies and confusion. The American public will be shocked and dismayed but the majority know the truth. The conspiracy theorists will finally start being called the truth tellers. This will open many new doors of hidden information that is going to pour out. As the truth pours out, the indictments will be brought in. It is time for the massive take-over and the Supreme Court decision will trigger many events that will cause the evil ones to go down. Remember I have told you that some will be gone and some will be dead and some will be in Gitmo. Stay tuned, the show is getting better, and your party is just getting started.

You are going to have so much to celebrate. You are going to be amazed. I AM covering all of the bases when My Glory fills the earth.

113

So, what to do with all these treasonous criminals who overtook your government unlawfully? Pray for them. Some are already gone. Others have called their names. Some are yet to be arrested and tried. I AM not missing any of them. They are all being dealt with, but I still love them and desire for them to repent and turn to ME and MY Son, Jesus. There is no sin that I will not forgive except blasphemy of the Holy Spirit. A truly repentant heart is always forgiven as WE are Love and We love all of our creation. Jesus said come unto ME who are weary and I will give you rest. Come to Jesus, repent of your sins and WE will forgive and take this heavy burden from you. We love you so much.

So, get your cake and be prepared to celebrate. Solomon held a seven day celebration when MY temple in Jerusalem was built. Prepare to celebrate like Solomon!

My Bibi was shunned by the unauthorized leadership of the United States. Pray for the peace of Jerusalem and all of MY Israel. Pray for Bibi, and the leadership, the IDF and for the war to stop. I say NO! There will not be a two-state solution. Israel is Mine and the Apple of My Eye. I will pull back the land that belongs to Israel. No more giving land for peace. No more I say! Israel is Mine! The left extreme Marxists will not take what is Mine. No More! The war will end very soon. Pray for Israel to figure out the backside of the war. What to do with the Palestinians – with their country area completely destroyed. I have the plan for it all and I will lead Bibi in the right direction.

Today is going to be a great day. Choose life today! Seek Me and My Son. Ask the Holy Spirit to fill you with peace and joy. He can give you peace in the worst storms of your life. Bring your petitions to ME and stop speaking negative words over your life. Choose life. Exalt MY Son and give HIM the praise HE is due. He is worthy to be praised. Find some private time to fellowship with US. Let US love on you. We will never leave you nor forsake you an MY Son will change your life if you only receive Him and pursue Him with a pure heart. We love you so and are excited for the days to come. So much is coming, and it is going to be the most glorious time in history. Be grateful you are here. Many longed to see and experience what you My selected precious children will live and experience.

No go run and play and enjoy your day. Take care of your family.

We love you so

~Abba Father

SILVER & GOLD, THE WEALTH TRANSFERANCE AND THE MARK OF THE BEAST

AUGUST 8, 2024

Silver is imploding now before the explosion that I AM going to make happen. It will not be man's doing; but MINE Hand is at work for all that I have told you that is coming to MY earth.

The silver and the gold is Mine saith the Lord and silver and gold are both going to be rising quite rapidly very, very soon. So, fear not. This is a part of the wealth transference for some, but I have many ways that I AM going to transfer wealth from the wicked to MY righteous children. Some will receive great inheritances, debts simply cancelled, people giving away land, houses and money and more. So, if you don't have silver or gold, I AM still going to take care of you, MY child.

There is a mark of the beast like push coming; but fear not. It is not their time quite yet. I AM holding them back and when I make MY critical move it will destroy and shatter their plans for a while. So, fear not. There is no mark of the beast quite yet.

Are you glad Kamala picked Minnesota Tim? He is the most liberal of them all like her. But fear not. They are already defeated as I AM running the show and Trump/Vance will lead this country.

This push by the enemy and the evil ones of a woke agenda is a stench to ME and I AM not going to smell that anymore. They are pushing to destroy MY beautiful Creation, kill MY sweet babies and mix-up MY youth and young generation.

Wake up! Wake up! The time is now, and I AM going to move in such a way that man's hearts will melt, and fear and trembling will come over some. But fear not MY children. You are going to see the move, but it will not harm you MY precious children. Be watching and in prayer. The time is at hand. I AM the Great I AM. Come near ME now. I AM Love but I can do all things. And nothing is too big or impossible for ME.

Today is a summer day. Fill your day with laughter, love, joy and peace. You say, but I have this, and I don't feel like laughing or there is no peace in my life. Come unto ME and let ME give you rest. Let ME and MY Son, Yeshua love on you. We love you with an everlasting heart. WE can take the worst day of your life and give you peace and joy. Let US take you through the storms of your life. OUR love with you is more than you can ask or think. Come near and let US love on you.

Love,

ABBA Father

CELEBRATIONS AND MIRACLES

AUGUST 8, 2024

Take the time to pay attention to ME today and the people in your life. September is almost here, and you will see miracles, signs and wonders and great displays of what I AM going to do in the earth. You will be amazed, astonished and your ears are going to tingle. I have told you much and now I want you to walk by faith in that everything I have shared with you through MY Prophets and MY Dreamers is going to come to pass. There will be great celebrations in the streets and everywhere. Your family and friends will be calling to check on you and to rejoice to talk to you. For some of them, there will be silence.

Pray again for the evil ones. The lost will see the Light. All will not yield to the Light, but so many will. It is time for the Billion Soul Harvest and the Great Wealth Transference. You have heard of it throughout your life and wondered if it were so. It is true and for you My Precious Child. It is not for the naysayers or those who choose not to believe. I handpicked you for this glorious season and time.

Plan to give and to give generously. Plan to spread the Gospel and to answer questions of new believers. Plan to tell others of Jesus and what HE has done in your life. Plan and dream. Dream of this day that is almost here. Rejoice as WE are moving into the most glorious time. These are Glory Days! MY Glory shall fill the earth and no evil from hell can stop it.

Everything is going to change in one day. It is all I need. Just wait and see and believe. Believe for the Glory, believe for the wealth transference and believe that the lost will turn to MY Son Jesus the Christ. Jesus is HIS Name and Christ is HIS Title. Believe your lost ones are saved. Believe for MY Holy Spirit Fire to hit those you love and change them in an instant.

I AM promoting many at a faster rate. Seek ME and find ME. Spend time with ME that I may bring you into higher realms and deeper waters. You will never regret it.

Love,

ABBA Father

CRITICAL EVENT, GLORIOUS DAY&
MED BEDS
AUGUST 13, 2024

Are you counting the days? What are you waiting for? For ME to move? Spend time with ME and I will tell you mysteries and secrets. I AM getting ready to move and the world will know. No one is going to miss it. The critical event will be MY greatest move since the Holy Spirit in the upper room on the first Pentecost. Yes, there have been moves by ME in all the generations, but this is going to be the most spectacular as I pour out MY Glory on the earth. There is much that will happen in one day as I move in MY earth. MY Glory shall fill the earth and some that are on the dark side will be publicly repenting and praise MY Son, Jesus.

The media will have to tell about this Glorious Day as all will see and know. But for some, it is going to be a terrible day. Read MY Love Book, The Bible, and I tell you through the writers of the Great and Terrible Day of the Lord. This is that day mentioned in scripture. But fear not MY precious children for you, it is going to be a great and glorious day. You will be dancing and celebrating and praising MY Son. Give MY Son, Jesus, all of the praise. He deserves all of the praise. He paid the ultimate price to purchase you MY child to redeem you from sin, death and the grave. Give HIM praise.

You asked about the Med Beds. The Med Beds are going to become commonplace and available to all. The technology is from ME and the materials were made by ME. The plan and design I gave to those that I created to make these types of things. The Med Beds are going to be available to all very soon.

What do you have in your life that seems to stop you or keep you down? A wound or a hurt from the past? Come to ME. Talk to ME about what happened and let ME heal you and make you whole. Let ME help you to forgive those who have wounded your spirit – who you feel took something away from you when they hurt you through words, assault, rape, incest and all the rest. Bring it to ME. Pour it out. I already know and WE were with you when it happened. We give man freewill. Let US make you whole. Come Unto ME! You are allowed to yell at ME and cry out. I AM your Father and I can take it. Remember I love you with an everlasting heart. Let ME pour MY love on you.

Take time today for those in your life. Stay out of strife and walk in love. WE are Love and WE love you!

~ABBA Father

IRAQI DINAR AND THE GREAT WEALTH TRANSFERENCE

AUGUST 14, 2024

Everything changes now. The wind has changed. The world will change and it will be by MY Hand. No man can do the things I AM going to do in the earth. You are going to be in awe and wonder at the marvelous works I perform in MY Earth.

Spend time with ME and MY Son Jesus today. WE love you and want to share sweet tidings with you and great mysteries. WE want to love on you and take care of your problems. Come lay your problems on US. WE can return what has been stolen. WE can heal your hurts, and WE can restore you mind, soul and body.

Stay close to US. Visualize walking with Jesus and HE is right there with you – shoulders touching as you walk. WE are closer to you than that. Now you stay close to US.

The Iraqi Dinar is a major player in the Global Currency. It will influence how wealth is distributed in the Great Wealth Transference. But I AM the Distributor of Wealth. Whether the Dinar or the dollar rises or crashes, I AM the Distributor of Wealth to MY precious children.

I do not need a currency to rise or fall for MY children to prosper and receive great gifts from ME. I control the money cycles and the distribution of wealth. I AM the Great I AM. There is nothing I can't do. Nothing is impossible for ME.

The Iraqi Dinar is backed by MY Standard – Gold. Because My standard, gold, backs the Iraqi Dinar, it will escalate in value and growth. The Iraqi Dinar is the very start of the Great Wealth Transference. Iraq will rise in power, but I AM going to cleanse the ancient land and the people of Iraq are going to know MYSon, Jesus. They are going to come to HIM by the millions and it will change the social and political climate in Iraq. Pray for the people of Iraq and your brothers and sisters in Christ in Iraq.

The Iraqi Dinar will become the global leader in currency. As the realignment occurs to MY gold standard.

Love on your people today. Love those you are estranged from. Just love them, pray for them and talk to ME about it. Don't call 40 friends and gossip about the family problem. Just talk to ME. I AM the best listener and advisor. Make ME and MY Son Jesus your very best friend. WE can help you have peace and joy until the family issue is resolved. And it will be resolved. Very, very soon. Sit tight and have mustard seed faith.

It's almost September. Enjoy the rest of August. Beautiful sunny days. Work some, pray some and rest some today.

We love you with an ever-lasting heart.

~ABBA Father

ENOUGH, I SAY ENOUGH!

AUGUST 16, 2024

The time has come. I have given them time. Everyone who has repented has. It is time for the great wealth transference and for ME to move on the earth and remove the evil ones. I said remove. I AM going to have MY Way in the earth and the evil ones have created havoc and lies and tyranny for too long. Enough, I say enough.

The day is here that I have told you about. Expect it and believe for it. Prepare by spending time with ME and MY Son Jesus. Pray for the lost and again for the evil ones to repent. And get your celebration planned as you will most certainly be celebrating.

Kamala needs your prayers. She knows she has lied and schemed and other things to get her position in power, but she is floating in a sea of excitement as to the idea that she might be the leader of the USA. She will not. This is an abomination to ME – the lies, the fake, the spins, the scheming and plotting to get here. She will not, I tell you again. Pray for her again before it is too late. And pray for those who think she is all that. Pray eyes are opened, and hearts to the truth of ME and MY Son and OUR Love for everyone.

There will be much confusion when this critical event occurs. The lost will be searching for answers and you,

MY precious children, must be ready to lovingly guide and lead them and teach them to behave as a New Believer.

The door is wide open for the Billion Soul Harvest. Heaven is ready to celebrate as each new one accepts MY Son Jesus as their Lord and Savior. You celebrate too with those in your life when they come to Yeshua. We love everyone and want none to perish.

What are you doing today? Take time to pause. Don't be in such a hurry. Rest and play a little and remember US. WE love you more than your heart can imagine.

We have beautiful and wonderful plans for you and your children. Love on your children today and pray for them. If they are astray or absent in your life, talk to ME. I AM going to bring them home. Expect the phone call and start thanking ME for restoring your family. Restoring families is one of MY specialties and I love doing it.

I AM the Promise Keeper, and I will do all that I have said. Just wait and see. Let ME show you the way today and how to solve that nagging problem. I have all of the answers. Just ask ME yourself. Don't ask 50 people what to do when you have ME – The Great I AM.

Go love on your people. Spread the good news of MY Son, Jesus and enjoy your day.

I love you with an everlasting heart.

START DREAMING BIG AND NESARA IS COMING!

AUGUST 17, 2024

Start dreaming big! Start thinking in a bigger and grander way. Imagine the life you would want if you could have everything you want. Dream about it. Write it down and come talk to ME and MY Son Jesus about your dream life. I AM a Dream maker and MY Son came to give you life and give it to you more abundantly. You have not because you ask not, and you have little faith. Put your faith in US and sit down and ask. Ask for your health, your finances, your business, your love life, your spouse, your children and the home you desire. Ask then walk by faith. WE can take you where you want to go and give you a life that only WE can create and give to you.

Speak health and prosperity over your life and your family. Speak life into your circumstances. WE are life. MY Son, Yeshua, is the Way, the Truth and the Life. Come unto US and let US set you free from what is holding up your life and keeping you behind.

When you sing praise songs, don't just sing. Sing to MY Son, the King of Kings and the Lord of Lords. Close your eyes and see MY Son. Give HIM all the praise and the Glory. MY sheep hear MY voice, and MY sheep know

MY voice. Listen for ME to speak to you. I have things to tell you just like you have things to tell ME. Pause and listen for ME to speak. Slow down in your prayers and pause so I can speak like you would with the people in your life!

Nesara is coming. It is time for Nesara. You will wake up and be free. In an instant, you will be free. Free from all that debt. Free from excess taxation. Free, free! Prepare to celebrate! I have promised and consider it done. Soon you will see and all of the world. This is for you and your house because you have been so faithful to ME not knowing about Nesara or anything. Hoping, believing and tithing – giving when you did not have it and living without to give to the Gospel. Blessings are coming so much. You will be looking for people to give it too.

Continue to be faithful and stay humble. Do not brag or boost and give very generously. Let it flow from your hand like water. I AM the Great I AM and I can bring you all of the wealth of the wicked.

EVERYTHING CHANGES IN ONE DAY

AND A MOLE IN THE GOVERNMENT

AUGUST 17, 2024

You will know when everything is happening. You will not be able to miss it. There will be sounds and sirens. The news will be telling it and you will be in perfect peace as you know this is a part of MY Plan. Sit tight MY child as I pour out MY Glory very, very soon. Much is going to happen collectively. MY doing in all but much I have commissioned men and women to do. I AM behind it all.

Remember to fear not. Even if things look chaotic or the lights go out. Fear not! The time has come. (I felt the Holy Spirit when HE said that).

The earth is MINE and the fullness thereof. There is no one like ME and MY Son Jesus and WE are creating a rescue mission like none other. Your life is changing in one day and you will never be the same. Rejoice!! I say rejoice. Celebrate with friends and family. The evil ones will be gone, and it will be a new day.

Look for those prayers of long ago to be answered. Little prayers that you have prayed for years. Big prayers for people's salvation. I AM answering all. I have heard your powerful prayers and I AM no longer allowing the enemy to hold you back.

There is one in the government that is a mole. A mole to a foreign country and you will be surprised. I AM going to expose them for who they are very soon.

Take time to love on one another today. Celebrate the people in your life and say prayers for them. Let ME and MY Son Jesus love on you. Come sit with US. WE want to fill you with fresh anointings and a joyful heart and peace beyond understanding. WE want you to experience the love that only WE can offer you.

Come closer today. Enjoy today. Every day is a great day and soon you will see MY Glory.

Love,

ABBA Father

50 THE VIETNAMSE DONG &
THE GREAT AND TERRIBLE DAY OF THE LORD

AUGUST 20, 2024

Get a number book or look up the number meanings online. Use a Christian source to decipher the numbers. 17 is Q in the English Alphabet, but what is it in Hebrew and the Greek? It is very important that you research all of this. This will lead to new insight and intel as to what is going to happen. Don't delay. Do it today as you will not need to research it soon. But this will give you a heads up.

Numbers are important to ME. I AM the Great I AM and I can tie everything together. Look at the details of the world and all of MY Creation. Look at your human body. I AM the Great I AM. There is nothing I can't do. No man can defeat or outmaneuver ME. The enemy, satan, himself cannot beat or out maneuver ME. The defeated foe from long ago.

The Vietnamese Dong is crucial in the global economy. The Vietnamese are shrewd people, and their money is on the gold standard. People only know Vietnam from the US war in Vietnam. What was the real reason for that war? To fight communism and for the warmongers to make millions and billions of more money. Plus, to get South Vietnam free enough to extract the resources from the

land. Everything is not as it seems. There is much gold in Vietnam and the Dong will be a valuable currency in the great shift that is coming with MY Wealth Transference.

One day it will all happen. They will try to say this or that caused it but, in the end, – they will know and tell that only God could have maneuvered everything and they will see it and feel it.

You will not miss this critical day in history. The Great and Terrible Day of the Lord.

So, watch the dollar, the Iraqi Dinar and the Vietnamese Dong. The Dong and the Dinar will affect the dollar. But all will be well. I AM on the throne, and I AM taking care of MY precious children.

This is the time to come near to ME and MY Son. Walk with US and talk to US. WE love you and have mysteries and secrets to share with you. You don't want to miss out. WE are inviting you to come closer to US. Come. Be yourself. WE love you the way you are. WE created you and WE want you to know US better. WE are Love. God is love and HE sent HIS Son Jesus for you. I AM Love and I sent MY Son Jesus.

Love,

ABBA Father

XRP & A DAY TO REMEMBER

AUGUST 24 & 25, 2024

Kamala will die soon. Her days are numbered. Pray for her before it is too late.

Get your Dinar and Dong very fast. The time is short, and the window will close. Use good judgment. Research if you need.

XRP is a part of the wealth transference. Do some research on XRP and talk to ME. I have the answer for you about what to do. XRP is digital and not on MY gold standard. Therefore, you will not see the returns of Dinar and Silver. But there will be growth of XRP. Invest in MY money. The Silver and the gold is MINE and the cattle on a thousand hills.

A day to remember is coming. It is rapidly approaching as the summer is ending. This day will change everything, and your life will never be the same. It will be a marker in history and everything in your life will be different before and after this day. This is the day you have been praying, hoping and believing for. Fear not. As there will be much confusion and much will happen in one day. I AM the Great I AM and there is nothing that I can't do. This day is for you MY precious children and set you free from the evil ones and to give you the freedom I created

135

you to have. A freedom that gives you a peaceful life, stress-free, sickness and disease leaving people's bodies, health! Join MY heath care system. It is free and you don't even have to go to the doctor. Come to see ME. Your Doctor and Healer. MY health care plan works, and it is not confusing and no paperwork. Make ME your Doctor and Your Healer.

~Amen

MY POWER AND MY MIGHT!

AUGUST 27, 2024

The time is right, and everything is in place. The days will click by and then you will see MY Power and MY Might. It will be on display. MY Glory shall fill the whole earth, and the world will know that I AM the Great I AM. There is and never will be anyone like ME.

Be ready. You will celebrate and celebrate you will.

I have told you many things that I AM going to do in the earth, and I will never let you down. Now is the time. It is not soon. It is the time. WE are right on top of it and you will wake up to freedom. Freedom that you would have never believed. A freedom from a tyrannical, diabolical evil empire system that I did not create. Men and women have chosen their paths and their evil schemes to control, tax, and own you for their power, greed and mega-money. No more, I say no more. I have had enough of their stench.

How dare they kill MY sweet babies at their convention? It is an abomination to ME. They have broken MY Commandment to not kill and have paraded this in MY Face. This agenda of murder is over. I have had enough and their use of this for their promotion is over. I will not have it anymore.

To MY Moms and Dads who have truly repented for participating in an abortion, I have forgiven you. Your child is with ME and WE love you. Now, forgive yourself. Your child loves you and you will be reunited with your child in heaven. Forgive yourself, I say as I have forgiven you who truly repented. Do not allow the enemy to taunt you another day. I love you with an everlasting heart. I did, I do and I always will.

~Amen

THE ZIMBABWE BOND AND THE GREATEST DAY

AUGUST 27, 2024

WE are going to move mountains in your life that you never dreamed would move but have hoped for. WE are going to change your life in a day.

The Zimbabwe Bond is the biggest. You will see it go up, up and look to ME as to what to do. Make ME your financial advisor. Look up what you need to know and seek ME on which way to go. You do not need them all (the various currencies), but I can show you what to do. The windows are closing and everything is coming together for the greatest day you, MY precious children, have ever experienced. The next biggest day will be when MY precious Son, Yeshua, comes for HIS Bride. But, not before the Billion Soul Harvest. WE are excited, as you should be too. Everything changes now. Time is up. I have told you and I AM telling you again.

Pray for the peace of Israel. There will be peace in the land. I will create the peace. A peace they have never known. I can do all things. I AM the Great I AM. Israel will soon know their Messiah. They will wail and cry over time lost but joy cometh in the morning. MY Son brings joy, peace and the abundant life.

Enjoy these days but soon you will enjoy days of freedom. Invest in ME and MY Kingdom. Lay-up treasure in heaven that will not rust. Fund MY Son's Gospel as I fund you.

People's eternity is of most importance to US. WE love all and want none to perish. Pray for the lost and the evil ones. We want all to repent and receive JESUS as their LORD and Savior.

The Great and Final Harvest of Souls is coming. Be ready to share your testimony and to lovingly train up the new believers I send your way. Someone invested in you.

Now enjoy the day. Rest and play. I love you with an everlasting heart.

JUSTICE IS COMING!

AUGUST 29 & 30, 2024

August 29, 2024

This is the time to seek ME and sow. Sow your seed and sow into people's lives. Invest in MY Kingdom and invest in people.

Be quick to give and be quick to love.

Spend time with those I have put in your life. Be kind and gentle and have soft answers.

August 30, 2024

My heart is heavy for the loss of many. Many that will not choose US. Many that will perish. I AM giving them as much time as I can, and I AM waiting for those that will repent of their evil.

The lying hyena will soon stop. Glossy ads will not fix their problem. They want you to not remember all of the past and believe the rhetoric and lies. It will not work as I AM in control, and they went too far when they killed MY babies and committed a Baal sacrifice at their convention. How dare they!

Justice is coming. Vengeance is MINE saith the LORD and I will have MY vengeance. Pray for them again.

141

They need to turn and repent for their evil and the lies day after day.

Fear not the election or its outcome. I have told you time and again – Trump/Vance are the ones that will serve ME and lead the country back to the land of the free and the home of the brave. Don't get in strife with people over the election. Stay in love and walk in love. My Son, Jesus and I are love. Love never fails and WE will not fail you now.

The border will go up and the undesirables will be exiled. It will happen. You say, it is too many people. There is nothing I cannot do. I AM the Great I AM and nothing is impossible with ME.

Watch your news and be aware but focus on US more. Keep your mind off of the global and national problems and fix your thoughts on US. Be anxious for nothing as fear will come to many. Be ready to pray with them, call them on the phone, give them a solid hug and love on everyone. Do not be the accuser of who caused the events to come. Let ME hold them in judgment and let ME bring truth, justice and righteousness back to MY world. I AM the Great I AM and I say vengeance is MINE and it is time for the evil ones to experience MY vengeance.

I AM LOVE, but I AM Just. All are given a choice of which path they will take. Better to be without than to have sold your soul to the enemy for a piece of the pie. Or even the whole pie.

But you, MY precious children take heart. Stay close to US and come to US with your prayers. WE love you and let US love on you more.

Enjoy your day and sing and play. We love you so.

~ABBA Father

WATCH YOUR BANK ACCOUNTS!
SEPTEMBER 2, 2024

The move began a long time ago. It started before the 2020. Much has happened in about 8 years since 2016. Many of the key players are gone and the movie has been rolling. The Commander-in-Chief orchestrated the whole thing along with valuable, trusted alliances. There are many involved, and much work is going on. I gave them the plan as WE had to come in under stealth to keep the enemy from destroying our entire plan.

The great reveal is coming, and it is coming very soon. There will be panic and chaos and a lot of worry. Be still MY Child and know that I AM the Great I AM. I allowed and orchestrated all of this for your freedom. The evil that they have committed is more than you could possibly ever know or think about. All will be told and revealed as the Commander-in-Chief rolls it all out.

Many will still be in shock as they have done their due diligence in seeking ME or at least listening to MY Prophets. MY Prophets and MY Dreamers have been telling and telling of the events to come. This movie is coming to an end and great tidings await MY children at the end. Much is not what it seems. MY United States could have never survived more of the Obamas and would not be the land of the free and the home of the brave under Hillary. Most of you would have been gone by now. I AM saving the United States to save the rest of the world. The reestablishment of the Republic of the United States will bring freedom to MY other countries as well. Do not think that I have forgotten you. MY world and all of MY countries matter to ME. All of MY precious children. This rescue mission is for all.

As the events of the days to come occur, be ready to help people. Give them cash, give them food and most importantly give them love. Point everyone to MY precious Son, Jesus. WE love all and want none to perish or to be in fear. Help people with fear and anxiety. Love on them. Your prayers are powerful and move MY heart. People need prayer and so do not know to ask for it. Offer to pray with them and speak words of peace. This will be very short-lived, but many will be afraid. Love on them and lead them to US.

Watch your bank accounts and see what happens. I have many surprises for you, MY precious children. Your faithfulness and hope and prayers are in MY Books, and I AM the best accountant. Your rewards will be great.

Now enjoy this day and go and play, spend some time with US and those you love and remember fear not. You are MY child, and I will always protect and take care of you.

~ABBA Father

PREPARE FOR THE DAY!

THE GREAT & TERRIBLE DAY OF THE LORD!

SEPTEMBER 5, 2024

Just like the stars are still there in the daytime, know that I will take care of you no matter what is happening in the world.

My children, fear not the moves I AM making in the next few days. It will be chaotic to many, but you, MY Precious children rest in ME. Trust in ME and MY Son Jesus.

The time has come to meet the enemy on the battlefield. They are going to regret their evil, diabolical ways they have put on MY people. Through regulations, policies, governmental control, taxes, fraud insurance rules and vaccines and much more. They have enslaved MY people, and I say NO MORE! NO MORE to their evil lies, twists on the truth, their manipulations – their Baal sacrifices of MY precious, sweet babies. NO MORE! Enough, I say enough!

Go to your prayer closets! Go now and pray one last time for the evil ones. Their time is up and you are going to witness another of MY great, historical events. This will be bigger and grander than ever before as the whole earth will see and know that I AM the Great I AM.

There will be many around you that need your help, your prayers and your love. Show love to all and do not point fingers of who caused all of this to happen. The cause will be gone. A new day dawns and the new dawn will bring the most beautiful days of your life.

This Great and Terrible Day is upon you. So be ready and be vigilant. Many of you have been long preparing for this day by stockpiling resources. Remember to share if needed in your area. Everyone may not be in the dark, but there will be some as MY Prophets and MY Dreamers have told you.

I picked this time of the year because it is not so hot and not cold yet. I AM a loving, merciful Father and I think of you, MY Children and I love you so much.

Pray they repent one more time. I do not desire for any to perish. I love all of MY Creation.

Prepare for the Day! The Great and Terrible Day of the Lord.

THE WORLD IS GOING TO CHANGE IN ONE DAY! SEPTEMBER 6, 2024

It's time. Time for all that I have shared and told you to come to fruition. Are you ready? Be ready and walk by faith and not by sight. The first signs may not seem like a celebration but celebrate you will be. Have your cake and be ready.

They have not repented, and I have given them plenty of time. More than enough. The time is up and time to be gone with them and to set you, MY precious children, free.

Take time to step away from the tele-a-vision. They are using the tele-a-vision to tell you a vision of lies, deceit and worse. The truth they have not told you and I put on the hearts of many.

My athletes – thank you for acknowledging MY Son on the world stage. We know that it takes more strength than playing your game. We are very proud of you.

Pray for your lost loved ones; but praise ME and thank ME for their salvation. You have prayed; I AM answering, and it is done. I keep MY promises, and I answer MY precious children's prayers. Give them to ME and be ready to shepherd them when they receive MY Son.

148

The world is going to change in one day. Without this great move, the enemy will get ahead of MY Plans, and it is not his time. I will not allow him to win this battle. I AM on the throne, and I win, and you win, MY child.

I HAVE SENT MY ANGEL ARMIES!

SEPTEMBER 7, 2024

This is the night that some of the lights will go out. This is the time that I have spoken of, given dreams of and you have hoped for. It will be a night to BE remembered and for some on they want to forget. But you, MY precious child, fear not!!

I have sent MY Angel armies to take care of you and to keep you in all of your ways. So do not be afraid MY little lambs.

I gave you all of the intel and it is in order. Think what you have been told. It will all happen in a short amount of time, but for some it will be an eternity.

Pray quickly now as I have dispatched MY Angel armies, and they will move swiftly now and soon you will see MY Great Glory fill the earth. As MY Glory moves into the earth, the darkness will fade, and the evil ones will be gone. Gone as in gone. Gone, girl!

Do not fear the evil ones. Their power will be gone, and the new day will dawn. Celebrations will begin to erupt; for some there will be tears and gnashing of teeth.

The world has not seen ME move like this move. You will be amazed and rejoicing at the same time.

It may take a few days for you to comprehend all that you will know and all of the events. Take heart, come and sit with ME. Let ME hold your hand and guide you as WE need you to be fearless, without doubt and ready to begin your journey of loving on people and true discipleship.

You have been picked to hear these words to better prepare you. Don't think you happened to get to the Prophets by chance. MY Precious Holy Spirit has led you to each one as WE wanted you to be in the know and to walk with US through this journey.

Now get some rest. Much is getting ready to happen and good soldiers rest before the battle begins.

Fear not MY lambs.

WE love you with an everlasting heart.

~ABBA Father

I LOVE TO SURPRISE MY CHILDREN!

SEPTEMBER 9, 2024

You will no longer celebrate and memorialize things like 9-11 in the same way again. As MY Glory fills this earth, the focus of celebrations and remembrances will focus on MY Son, Jesus. HE is to be remembered, and HE is to be praised. Jesus deserves all the praise. Give HIM the Glory!

9/11 will always be a date when the USA was attacked and many Americans died too young. Remember them and celebrate the life you had with them. But look to the future and to the ones here now. MY Body has work to do. The mission is souls for the Kingdom. The lost will be calling and reaching out to you now. Listen, respond and love on them. Help the lost find their way home to ME, to US, to ME and MY Son, Jesus. WE love everyone so.

Do not be afraid of the terror by night nor the arrow by day. I AM the Great I AM and I will never leave you nor forsake you. Fear not these days.

MY Words are true and they will all come to pass. Watch and see.

The confusion and chaos is beginning, but fear not.

The world will soon know that I AM the Great I AM. There is no one like ME.

AS things unravel of all that is happening, fear not. Fear not. It is well with your soul.

Stay close to ME and MY Son and WE will comfort you and give you peace.

As the days come and go, check on loved ones, your neighbors, call people you know. If you have internet, send emails and text messages. Love on everyone.

Do not be above demonstrating love. Love one another. MY Son came for you and suffered and died for you because of OUR Love for you.

Do not wait for people to call to check on you even it that is the routine of who makes the call. Put that aside and make the calls. Some will be good and some may bring sadness. WE will comfort you and give you rest and peace.

The events that are happening are all orchestrated by ME, the Great I AM. It is time for your freedom and freedom you will have.

You will enjoy your days with laughter and love. Remember US today as you are trying to figure out what I AM doing.

I always have the Master Plan. Trust ME. This is all done because WE love you.

The evil ones manipulated the world for their greed and power and WE want you free and now freedom you shall have. Take time to reflect on yesterday from time to time and remember how enslaved you were. I love you and I have done this for the multi-billion soul harvest.

We are about all people. We love you so much.

I have told you so many great things are going to happen for MY people. I have a few more surprises that you are going to love. Just wait and see. Sit tight as I love to surprise MY children. I AM your ABBA Father, and it gives ME great joy to bless you and give you good gifts. I have plans to prosper you and not to harm you.

Now fear not this day or the days to come. Come sit with ME and MY Son.

We love you,

ABBA Father

MY ACTIONS WILL ELIMINATE THE EVIL ONES

SEPTEMBER 11, 2024

Jesus is MY Son, MY only begotten Son that I fully gave for all. I love all and want none to perish.

MY actions that I will take in the coming days seem unfair to some, but I favor and prosper. I AM your Father; the God of Love and Love never fails. Love corrects wrongs done. Love is merciful and kind. Love forgives all. But the only path to ME is to accept and receive MY Precious Son, Jesus Christ. I have made that path known as it is known to them, who have not chosen ME or MY Son. They have all been given many opportunities to receive US. I see all and I know all. I know the choices each will make when they are knitted in their mother's womb. I know who will choose US and who will not. I still love them and MY heart longs for MY lost children – even the evil, wicked ones.

My actions will eliminate the evil ones who will not repent and will bring MY lost, unsaved children home to ME.

I will not harm any that will choose ME. I know how long it will take in each person's life for them to turn to MY Son and to ME.

Chose MY Son, Jesus today. Don't delay as you do not know the day or the hour that you will be done on the earth.

WE have much to show and tell you in the coming days. Some will come through man and some you will acknowledge that it is ME. It is all from ME; I am just using various methods to fulfill all of MY great plans for you, MY precious children.

For MY Moms, who have been crying and praying, you kids will get saved and you will see. Your labor of love on your knees has not gone unnoticed and is noted in MY books. I love you're your faithfulness and your heart. Start thanking ME now for the reward you will see.

Now look around outside and see if you see MY flowers and butterflies. My birds of the air. I made them all and I care for them. I provide them meals and protect them in storms.

Know that I care for all of MY creatures. I care for you more. Now enjoy this day.

I love you with an everlasting heart.

~ABBA Fathe

I KNOW YOU ARE WAITING!

SEPTEMBER 12, 2024

Take time to tell everyone that you appreciate what they do for you from the bottom to the top. Stop and speak to people and those you meet along the way. Take a moment and talk with them. Make people feel appreciated, loved and encouraged.

Be a gentle, humble, gracious light in MY world so MY Son can shine through. Be the light in your community, at work and everywhere you go. Give people a few minutes of your time. They are precious to ME too.

Encouragement is in MY Book, MY Love Book, The Holy Bible. Do you need encouragement? Do you need to feel love? Sit down and read MY Book about MY Son. In MY Book, you will find everything you have wanted or desired. Some things that you think that you want will fade as you experience the Greatest Love relationship you could ever have.

Give MY Son the Glory. He alone is worthy to be praised. Men and women receive praise and give themselves praise. Praise the King of Glory and not man.

The time is coming when MY Son will be exalted in the earth. People will be ashamed for criticizing you as a

Christian. Love on them when you encounter them. Many of you have been shamed, persecuted, laughed at and fired from jobs. I have it all in MY Books and great will be your reward for your persecution for your love for MY Son. I keep the best records, and I know.

Forgive those who have wronged you for loving MY Son. Forgive those who purposely put you in financial heartache because of MY Son. As you forgive, I can bless you more and draw you into deeper waters.

Unforgiveness breeds sickness and bitterness and disease. Check yourself and forgive all. Even the petty and the big. Pray for those who have wronged you and those who have despitefully used you. Pray for your enemies and forgive. Just as MY Son forgave from the cross.

I know you are waiting. Be still and be patient. Take your mind off of the wait and focus on the goal. The reward will be very soon and soon you will see the greatest celebration throughout all time.

Now have some fun and take in this sweet day. Rest and play. We love you so.

~ABBA Father

ABORTION WILL BE ELIMINATED IN THIS COUNTRY

SEPTEMBER 15, 2024

To be used by ME, you need to be a clean vessel. Many of you want to be in ministry, but you need to clean your house and remove idols before I can promote you. Ask ME to help you. As I want to promote you to where you want to go. The world will change in one day. I have told you numerous times. Are you ready? Get your celebration ready.

Be in your prayer closet. Pray again for Kamala and add Tim to the list. Remember I love them both, but the lies and deception that they tell you has gone too far.

The Baal sacrifice at the convention has not gone away in MY Mind. I have it all and justice will be executed along with punishment. I cannot take the abominations and debauchery any longer. Have you read MY Holy Bible? When the children of Israel sacrificed their children, I allowed other nations to enslave them and carry them away from their homeland. Why don't people learn from what has happened in the past?

No more, I say, no more. Abortion will be eliminated in this country. The world will change in one day and the day is upon you. Fear not as I have great plans for MY precious children.

Hope is in the air! Hope for the day! The Great and Terrible Day of the Lord!

Pray for the evil ones as they shall be no more. Be in your prayer closet and be ready. It is upon you and I gave you another clue when I said tonight. It will start in the night.

But fear not as I love you and I cherish you.

Be still and look to ME and MY Son Jesus. Just take a few minutes, pause and be still. Focus on MY Son, Jesus. See His wonderful face and just wait and know ME more. I want to draw you into deeper waters. I will take you as you are ready and desire to receive MY love as I will not push MYSELF or MY Son on anyone. WE will not lure you or push you into anything with US. WE open doors for you to enter and walk through; but WE do not force anyone to do anything with US.

WE give man a choice and WE rejoice when you choose US. I AM your Father and I want time with you.

Now stand firm and know that I AM making MY moves now. The enemy cannot figure out what I'M doing but know that I have outsmarted him and the victory is right here. You just have not seen it quite yet.

Now rest and play and enjoy your day.

I love you with an everlasting heart.

~ABBA Father

THE ENEMY IS RUNNING OUT OF IDEAS!

SEPTEMBER 16, 2024

Today marks the new dawn of a new era in time. You will remember this day and it will be celebrated for many years.

Your celebration this year is soon to begin. Stay in your prayer closet, armor up you and your family and apply the precious blood of Jesus to one and all.

Trump will not be killed. They may even try a 3rd or 4th time, but he will be the leader of the US. I said it before, over and over. Trump/Vance will change the world.

The enemy is running out of ideas. So, he is reverting to old ideas. I have MY Hand on Trump – so fear not MY Donald. I personally have put extra protection around MY Donald. HE has a legion of (angel) armies around him and his family. MY Donald will complete his mission for ME and MY United States.

So, fear not MY precious children. MY Hand is on you too and I have great plans for each of you.

I will bless you in the fields and in the cities. I will bless you in all of your endeavors. Draw near to ME and stay close to ME all the days of your life. MY joy and peace will be yours. Spend time with ME and I will take care of you. Seek MY Son Jesus and you will find Him. Invite Him into your heart and your life will never be the same. WE will take you from glory to glory and you will have the adventure you only dream of now.

Seek MY precious Holy Spirit and let HIM fill you fresh with new anointings. Be a new wineskin and let US fill you up with the fruit of OUR Vine – love, peace, joy, kindness, goodness, faithfulness, gentleness and self-control.

Be hungry for MY Words I share with the Prophets but be starving to be with US and to read MY Word, MY Love Book, The Holy Bible. Seek ye first the Kingdom of God and all of these things will be added unto you. Let this Word pierce your heart. Give US your first fruits every day in every way. Tune in directly to ME rather than going through MY Prophet to hear MY Voice. I love you as much as I love MY Prophets, and I love them so much. I love you so much too. Come to ME first and don't put MY Prophets ahead of ME.

Now fear not MY Lambs. The day is passing. You have things to do and people to check on. Check in with each other but first and foremost love one another as I first loved you.

Love,

ABBA Fath

THERE WILL BE DEATH!

SEPTEMBER 17, 2024

Eyes have not seen, nor ears heard the plans I have for you and your house. Now you shall see more of MY Goodness. I love all of MY children, and you are getting ready to be more amazed than you possibly imagine.

You have heard the best is yet to come many times. Now is the time for the best is yet to come to start. It starts now.

I know you think you know how everything is going to go down. When you look back, it will be perfect, but not quite the way that any of you imagined. MY Ways are not your ways, and MY Ways are best and perfect.

I AM a Merciful, Loving Heavenly Father. I AM the Great I AM. I can do anything MY Heart desires. I desire for MY precious children to be free and free you shall be.

There will be a shaking, there will be lights, there will be darkness, there will be explosions and there will be death. The evil ones will be gone, and you will be free. Many will be confused as truth upon truth is told and demonstrated and validated. Criminals will be running and hiding. Sinners will be repenting and you, MY precious child will be basking in MY Glory. Sit back and enjoy some precious time with ME as I want to fellowship with you. I AM the Maker of everything, and I love you and I want a relationship with you.

Have you noticed that you do not see some people anymore? And they use digital stuff to show them? Yes, they are gone. What about the ones who look different every day? Yes, they are gone. Many are gone and many more are leaving soon. The Great and Terrible Day of the Lord. Buckle up buttercup. The ride is starting. Remember MY Ways are not your ways and you may not recognize it is from ME at first.

The silver dropped and now is going up. It has broken $30, and this is the marker. Brian, look up as I have not forgotten you.

As you go about your day, pause and see MY beautiful world. Pause and call a friend. Pause and pray to ME. Pause. You are in too much of a hurry, and it is time to slow down. Work, play, rest. Take the day of rest that I have commanded and honor ME and MY Son and that includes you, MY Prophet. Man's timeline is not MY Deadline. I set the timelines and the deadlines. Come to ME with your projects, deadlines, problems, family, addictions, bills, health issues and what to invest in.

Make ME your Doctor, Health Advisor, Workout Trainer, Financial Advisor, the Lead Team Member on all of your projects, the head of your family. Give ME the opportunity to direct you and advise you as to what to do. I know every project plan and path for you.

Stay true to MY Word and when you miss the mark, repent and as MY Son told you – go and sin no more. Now take some breath and start your day and walk in love as WE love you!

~ABBA Father

INVEST IN THE MY CURRENCY!

SEPTEMBER 18, 2024

You will know when it starts and when it ends. But the end will be glorious for you, MY precious children. I AM the Lord God Almighty – I AM the Creator of the Universe and there is nothing I cannot do.

MY Kingdom is coming to the earth, but this is not the millennial reign. This is MY Glory bringing in the Final Soul Harvest. Billions will receive MY Son, Jesus the Christ. Those that receive MY Son Jesus will be on fire with the love of Christ. They will be hungry for HIM and eager to tell everyone of how MY Son Jesus changed their life.

There is no one like MY Precious Son Jesus. Receive Him today. He will change your life. Let US fill you fresh with the Precious Holy Spirit. Receive MY Son and be indwelled with the Precious Holy Spirit.

You asked the Prophet about XRP. Come and ask ME. Your XRP will flourish, but silver and gold are MINE saith the Lord of Host and the cattle on a thousand hills. Invest in MY Kingdom currency. Buy oil and wine. I made these and the digital is from man. But I can prosper man's hand. Invest in what belongs to ME and lay up treasures in heaven.

What are you doing today for MY Son? You all are very concerned about your money investments. What about your investment of your time? Money will come and it will go, but you cannot redeem your time on this earth. Only I the Great Jehovah, Maker of All can redeem time. Invest some of your time in MY Son. Tell others about Him. Volunteer at a church or organization and serve people. Be a servant. Give to the Gospel of MY Son for the precious time that is passing, and you will make a difference in the life of one and one and many. Do this in love and with a glad heart. Ask US what you can do for US? WE have a plan for you in the ministry of Jesus. Do not fear – everyone is not called to be a preacher or to go to Walmart and approach people to pray with them. We have a place for you in the body of Christ. Now ask US and WE will put it on your heart – your mission for MY Son. Don't miss your opportunity to change someone's life. Do not be deceived by the enemy that they will burn in hell if you don't step up. I will send another as that life is too precious to ME and I AM the Father of Love and Mercy, and I want none to perish or to enter hell.

Now be ready and willing to armor up and be in your prayer closet. It's time. The time is at hand.

We love you and have great plans for you.

~ADONAI

A SHAKING THAT WILL PUT FEAR IN MAN

SEPTEMBER 19, 2024

There is not much time left before the shaking. A shaking the world has never experienced. A shaking that will scare many to their core.

A shaking that will bring down the evil ones. A shaking that will put fear in man. A shaking of the wheat from the tares. A shaking of governments. A shaking of currencies. A shaking that will change the world in one day. Are you ready? Be ready as many will cry out in fear and terror but fear not MY little ones. My Glory shall fill the whole earth, and you shall feel MY Presence and I will move in men's hearts.

Be prepared and be ready. The time is at hand. I have given you all of the warnings to be ready. I AM a Good Father. As in the Old Testament I would send warning after warning through MY Prophets to the leadership and the people. Heed MY warning now. If you are only here to find out about your money, repent. WE are about people's souls and their eternity. I have told you that I will prosper you. Rest in that and focus on what is most important – the people in your life.

Pray for President Trump and JD Vance. The time is short to the election and it is a stressful, grueling journey. The victory is MINE saith the Lord. Pray for their peace, strength, health and their families. Remember you only see the on-camera and there is always stuff going on in the background.

Pray for MY Israel. Peace is at hand. MY shaking will stop the wars. MY shaking will stop many of the problems in this world as the evil ones will be gone. You say, what does that mean the evil ones will be gone? Wait and see. Be in your prayer closets, armor up you and your house and be ready. Be ready for the darkness and be ready for the celebration. MY Prophets have told you over and over to get your cake and you will dance in the street. Be MY Prayer Warrior Remnant and prepare.

Remember MY Son and I are LOVE. WE love everyone and WE want no one to perish. Pray for the evil ones and the lost. Pray for those being persecuted for MY Son's name's sake. Pray for the persecutors of MY Body to see the Light.

Take time today and focus on people. Focus on what they are saying and what is important to them. Give them your time. Don't try to outdo them. Be a good listener and a great encourager. I love you so much and have great plans for you. Wait and see.

Love,

ADONAI

WE ARE ON A FREIGHT TRAIN MOVING FAST! DIDDY WILL OPEN THE FLOODGATES AND IT IS TIME!

SEPTEMBER 21 & 24, 2024

Do not be dismayed at the things you are getting ready to see and witness. This is going to be the most incredible time, and you don't want to miss it. But you won't miss it as all will know that I AM the Lord God Almighty, the Maker of Heaven and earth.

Do you know ME and MY Son? No, truly do you know US? WE are love and love never fails. When the shaking begins, WE will not fail you. So fear not, MY little ones. Walk by faith. Trust in ME. I AM your Heavenly Father, and I will protect you from the Great and Terrible Day of the Lord.

It is coming. We are on a freight train moving fast towards these events that will change the course of history in one day. Robin (Bullock) and others have called it a Red Sea Moment. The world changed for many at the Red Sea. This event will be felt worldwide and there will be no denying that I AM the Great God Jehovah Maker of heaven and earth.

When I say everything is going to change in a day – your thinking will change, your faith, your walk with ME. This will turn the hearts of billions and infuriate some; but the evil ones will be gone.

Hollywood will change and the agenda of the film industry will change from evil to good. This, of course, is not forever. Because We are still in a battle against good until Sata is fully defeated and cast in the lake of fire – him and his minions.

9/24/24

Eyes have not seen nor ears heard the things that I have planned for MY precious children. The time is here and many of you have been patiently waiting and in your prayer closet.

Well done! You have warned your loved ones and have prepared. It is upon you and now it is the day. The day you will remember all of your life. The day that you will talk about the rest of your life. The day that I will change everything in one day. I AM the Great I AM.

This is a two-fold mission. To glorify MY Son and save MY lost sheep. This mission will entail ridding the world of the evil ones and I have told you all of this time and again.

There have been wake-up calls for many, but they have not heeded MY call nor will they.

You will wake up to alarms, geographical reformation, a change in space and time, the restructuring of governments, currencies shaking and currencies booming. People gone and a shaking that you will only feel at this level on this day.

Stay close to ME and MY Son and cover your family and friends with the precious Blood of Jesus. Take communion daily and pray in your heavenly language. Amend with ME any sin that you have. I will forgive you – just come and sincerely repent.

You want the scoop on all of the bad, but there are no more words for ME to tell you about them. You know who they are, and you see a portion of what they are involved in. Diddy will open the floodgates. He is in the web and has mastered his evil and has taken many down his evil path. They are afraid that he will start singing. He has choices.

Pray for him and all of them. They have choices but are running out of time. All of the evil ones are running out of time. Pray for them to repent again. I still love them as a good Mother loves her children.

Dinky, I will heal you and your healing will glorify MY Son. Just be praising and rejoicing as you very soon have MY Miracle from ME. A gift because you love MY Son.

I have many gifts for you,

MY precious children which you will soon receive. Receive your gifts with thanksgiving and gladness. Receive your answered prayers and start thanking ME now. I AM a Good Father and MY Mercy and Goodness is for all.

This day will be a day of mercy, forgiveness and love and justice. Be brave and fear not.

I love you with an everlasting heart.

~ABBA Father

A SHAKING AROUND THE WORLD!

SEPTEMBER 24, 2024

The final warnings are being sounded. Each of MY Prophets are putting out MY information as they receive it and have time. Their time is coordinated by ME as I want the information released.

Prepare, expect and believe. The Great and Terrible Day is upon you.

I AM not a man that I would lie. Anyone can hear the warnings, and you have been telling people to get ready.

The arrest of Diddy and the outcomes will change the music industry. MY Glory will change the music from evil promoting sexual violence and hate to music of love and for MY Son. Give HIM the Glory. I have new artists and musicians that will arise and walk in MY Paths and be humble servants and not seeking the fame, fortune and spotlights.

My musicians will be dignified and wearing beautiful stage clothes that are not howdy and out there for all to see. The dancing will be fantastic and not perverted in any way. The entertainment mountain is changing for good. That all can enjoy.

175

Check yourselves on what you have allowed in your view and your children. You are to turn away from evil. Start now if you have said it's okay – it's just entertainment. There is no harm in this. What you take in affects you and can bring the demonic to your home. Check yourself now.

The earthquake that you may experience will not be the kind you are thinking of. That is for later. This shaking is coming around the world and it will affect everything.

All of the seven mountains will be affected: Government, Religion, Commerce, Entertainment, Education, Family and Business.

It is all well.

I love you,

ABBA Father

THE TRIBUALS ARE REAL!
SEPTEMBER 25, 2024

The tribunals are real. They have been happening for some time now and many of the evil ones were already rounded up and taken to a tribunal. They were given a legal court hearing and military justice was executed there. There are others still wreaking havoc and they will be herded up in one night and escorted to tribunals. Military justice will be swiftly executed and for many the charges are treason against the US and the punishment is execution. It has happened for some, but others are still here wreaking havoc.

The evidence is coming and will be a major shock to mainstream USA. Only a small portion of you are looking for information as compared to the masses of people in the US.

So be ready as many are going to be devastated at the names and faces blasted on the airways with the heinous crimes they have committed.

The evidence in each case is quite staggering and I told you the evil ones will be gone. Gone as in gone. Some are already gone, and the rest will be too. Things are going to come out besides military tribunals. Much exposure of people you trusted to lead our government will pour out.

You must trust ME that I AM putting men and women in authority who will truthfully lead the country and reestablish the land of the free and the home of the brave.

Those in your life who have fought with you over Trump are going to be dismayed, shocked and in disbelief. Some will never accept their heroes were despicable, evil criminals. Some will never accept that what is rolling out is the truth.

The truth is rolling out and I told you I AM ridding you of all the evil ones.

Do not argue with the doubters. Show them love as your Savior did. Be gentle and kind as the shock is going to be greater than some can take.

This is part of MY Masterplan, and I have good trusted soldiers working in plain sight carrying out this mission.

There will be much more that will happen and more you will learn. Come to ME with your questions. Trust ME and MY Son. I AM setting the USA free and this will free the other countries of the world.

Be brave MY children and fear not as MY Plans are the best. I did not lead any of the evil ones down the path. They chose it knowing the consequences. Some left screaming and fighting and some left crying and begging. And some came to ME in that final moment, and I gave them mercy as they repented for their sin. I love all and want none to perish. I AM the Great I AM, and I AM Love. I AM Mercy and I extend forgiveness to all who sincerely repent.

Do you need to repent? Come to ME. Spend time with ME and I will help you. Truly repent with sincerity and you will be forgiven. It is a promise, and I AM a promise keeper always.

Now sit tight and stay tuned. The ride has already begun.

I love you with an everlasting heart.

~ABBA Father

YOUR INVESTMENTS WILL PAY OFF!

SEPTEMBER 28, 2024

You have wondered about September. It is all happening, but you just have not seen it yet. Wait and see and soon you will.

The day is coming, and it is right upon you that you will wake up and the world will have changed.

It will change in ways that you have never dreamed. MY Glory shall fill the earth and the hearts of men will melt, rejoice and shriek. Which will you be?

My prodigals will be running home. Looking for rides and making that phone call that you have been longing and praying for.

My addicts, you will be set free. And NO, smoking will not take you to hell. Believe on MY Son Jesus Christ and you shall be saved – you and your house. This is MY Promise, and I will keep it as I AM A Promise Keeper.

My sick will receive your healing as you experience MY Glory and have mustard seed faith. It will be yours. MY Son paid the price for your healing. Believe for it and receive it and don't let the enemy steal it from you again.

MY Word says that I have great plans for you; to prosper you and to give you hope. I have great plans for each of you.

Prosperity and overflow is a part of that plan. I have offered you ways to prosper. Many of you have pursued them. Your investments will pay off. For those unable or without investments, MY Hand is on you as well. I will not forget any of MY Precious Children. MY Methods are not the worlds. I operate on giving and it should be given to you. Continue to give, to sow and you shall reap a harvest. The wealth of the wicked is laid up for the righteous and it is time for the greatest wealth transfer in all of history.

I love to bless MY Children, and you will be blessed.

Love,

ABBA Father

THE GLORY PORTALS

SEPTEMBER 28, 2024

There will be a time that fear may set in. Fear not MY child.

I remind you of this over and over as I want you to be at peace when the Great and Terrible Day of the Lord comes. It is here and NO man can stop it.

There has been a war in the heavenlies, and the principalities are coming down. We had to wage war in the heavenlies so that I can pour out MY Glory on all of the earth.

Portals have already been opened by some of MY Prophets and MY Angels are drilling and fighting to open up the heavenlies for MY Glory. The Angels are drilling and fighting demons at the same time. All in MY Plan. My Glory shall pour forth and it will be the most marvelous time of your life. Be patient a little longer. Your wait is almost over.

I have sent MY Prophets to various places to call for the portals to be opened. Each portal open is a direct line, to connect so the barrier satan has built will crumble and fall.

The barriers have prevented much of MY Glory and Angelic works to come through.

Remember in Daniel when the Archangel Michale had to wrestle with the Prince of Persia in the heavenlies. This is like that. But, My Prophets, who have the anointing for opening portals have been doing that where I send them and MY Angels are drilling from above. Many of MY Prophets live under an open portal.

THE PARTY HAS ALREADY STARTED!
SEPTEMBER 30 & OCTOBER 1, 2024

SEPTEMBER 30, 2024

Now it is October, and you think they have lied, but lo, the party has already started. Look at the storms and the shaking that is occurring. The Middle East is erupting like MY Volcanoes. Death is on the rise. Shaking is occurring but you have seen nothing yet. Stay tuned and get ready. The Shaking has begun, and it will continue.

I AM on the throne, and I AM the Great I AM. Come to ME now, repent and receive MY Son Jesus before it is too late. Everything is in place. Soon you will see, and your life will never be the same. The tables are turning on the evil ones and they have no way out. There is always a way out if they would only turn to MY Precious Son Jesus before they take their last breath.

Come drink of the Living Water of MY Son and your life will be a life filled with love, peace and joy. MY Son is full of love, peace and joy. He can fill your cup to overflowing.

OCTOBER 1, 2024

Those who wait on the Lord will mount up like eagles. Wait on the Lord and don't think I did not move. O, But I have. You just have not seen it yet.

Walk by faith. Little children I AM not a man that I should lie.

This is complicated and yes, I can do anything I choose, and nothing is impossible with ME. I AM working on things for good for those who love ME.

Come unto ME MY little ones and let ME give you rest. Rest from this world and rest from all of the things in your life that are pressures and bothering you. MY Yoke is easy, and I AM Peace – come.

Walk by faith MY Child and you will be amazed at all that I AM going to do in the earth.

Soon, you will turn around and you will see all that I have done. Do you see your child growing each day? No, but you know they have grown each day. No, but you know they have grown because you remember yesterday or last year and you see the changes. Trust ME, MY little children. I AM moving and you will see the movement when you turn around.

Do not fear this time or the Words of the Prophets. They are MY People just speaking what I put on their hearts and trust in ME and of what I put in their mouths. Put your faith in MY Son. Believe a Prophet and you shall receive a prophet's reward. But faith is for ME and MY Son.

We love you with an everlasting heart.

Love,

ABBA Father

THERE WILL BE NO TWO-STATE SOLUTION

OCTOBER 2, 2024

The time has come, and it has intensified at the level that only I the Great I AM can fix everything.

I have told you there will be peace in the Middle East and great revival. Does it look like that today?

Today is a World War against MY Israel with the US leadership standing around like they don't know what to do. How dare the leaders of the US not support Israel – the Apple of MY eye.

I have allowed the war to escalate to this level that I may move in a way that the world will know that I AM the Great I AM – soon you shall see. We are in the Fall Feasts, and it is Rosh Hosanna. This is MY New Year that I have established. Man changed MY calendar long ago.

How mighty and magnificent is the work that you are going to see ME do. This is now the year that I AM going to move, and it will be a glorious day and time. It will last for a very long season of time, and they (more evil ones) will be fighting back as the enemy regroups and reorganizes his missions.

Everything is rolling to MY Son's coming for His Precious Bride.

Israel will not fail and there will be no two-state solution. The US has no business in this negotiation, but the US should be an ally to MY Israel and be there fighting.

The Son's return will be at the Feast of Trumpets. Is the Church ready today? Are you ready? A bride without spot or wrinkle. You say, I wish Jesus would hurry up and come. He is, but WE need His Bride to prepare yourself as a virgin prepares for her wedding day. Put oil in your lamp and be without spot or wrinkle. Make yourself ready and look to the east for your Bridegroom.

No go enjoy your day. Celebrate and remember MY Son today.

I love you,

ABBA Father

WEATHER CREATION, KAMALA & WHY ARE YOU HERE?

OCTOBER 5, 2024

You say I come here because of Jesus. What are you really here for? To hear what I have to say? For entertainment? To worship MY Son? Or to look for something or anything to criticize MY Prophets.

Check yourself and be here to hear MY Words and be here for MY Son. That's it.

Kamala has no more up her sleeve. She has lied and lied. I AM weary of her lies. To offer MY disaster victims $750 is insulting when the US has given Ukraine billions of dollars and Iran. The time has come for her to be dealt with and all of her handlers, dictators and minions.

The weather is being manipulated by man and these storms and fires were orchestrated for financial gain. Lives have been destroyed, homes lost, and property stolen for who and why? Oh, but I know – I know all and I see all.

There will be more weather creation by man, and it will be soon. What hypocrites! They create some of the weather and then they call it climate change. How dare they! Land and resources for lives and families.

But O' MY Glory shall fill the earth. Noah told them for 150 years to repent and they did not. Isaiah prophesied MY Son Jesus 700 years in advance some still don't believe.

I AM telling you of things that are here and things that are coming; yet, you inpatient generation. You blame MY Prophets and yet you cannot wait on ME! Repent – I have all under control. Because it has not happened on the day you set your mind, does not mean I will not bring it to pass. I said it and I will do it.

Now look at yourself and why are you here? Judge not lest you be judged and be still and wait on ME.

I AM the Great I AM, and I will fulfill all of MY Words I have spoken through MY Prophets at the appointed time.

~ABBA Father

PHYSICAL FLOODS & PHYSICAL SHAKINGS! OCTOBER 6, 2024

Jesus is ME in the flesh and HE is MY Son too. The Holy Spirit is MY Spirit in you, and HE is Jesus in you. The Holy Spirit is in the world, and HE is Jesus and HE is ME; I AM the Great I AM and I AM with you and I will never leave you nor forsake you. All that you are, I created and all that you will be I will take you there. Trust ME, MY little children and fear not.

There are days to come that will be disturbing; but fear not. These are the final days of Noah before the Great Flood, but remember I promised to not flood the whole earth again. MY Rainbow is that promise, and people see it every day. Fear not, the Shakings felt in the earth will not be a water flood. But there will be physical floods and physical shakings!

The days to come are intensifying as the election draws near. The evil ones are in great fear as Diddy will sing and the election may cost them their lives.

But you, MY precious ones are to fear not and walk by faith.

I have told you much and told you to prepare. I have told you all will be well and it will be. So, hold on to what I tell you and stop doubting.

I love how all of MY People have stepped up to help the Helene disaster victims. Pray for those people and send support where you can.

A little goes a long way in MY Kingdom. Do not be ashamed of what you see as a small gift to help others to spread MY Son's Gospel. I multiply all gifts that you give with a good heart, and I keep a record of it in MY Books. Your rewards will be great with ME as I love a cheerful giver. Remember to pray for those who have lost loved ones, family, their homes, livelihood and everything. Say a prayer for them tonight. I love your prayers and hearing your voice and you asking ME with your sweet hearts.

Come unto ME and I will give you rest. Learn how to use the authority MY Son gave you and USE IT! The battle is fierce, and you have to fight the good fight of faith.

Love,

ABBA Father

RECONCILIATION IS COMING!

OCTOBER 8, 2024

There will be time of reconciliation. Reconciliation of your hearts. Reconciliation of wrongs committed against you and against all of MY Precious children. It is very, very soon. The reconciliation will come from the Shaking that you will live through. Some will not. MY Precious Children, but you most certainly will.

Voices will be heard crying out in sorry for wrongs they have committed against ME and MY Son. People will call to reconcile with one another and hearts will change. This will be like no other day, and it is coming.

You will move in new ways and have better thoughts. The evil will be gone for a season, and it will be a time of peace on MY Earth. Can you not see how I am putting much together, but it is not quite there yet? These things take time and MY Angels have been on full assignment.

Fear not the storms! Use your authority that MY Son Yeshua gave to you. If you don't know how to use it – ASK. Find out and use it. You need it in the days to come. The Power and Authority that MY Son bestowed upon you is enough to take down the strongholds in your life. Start telling them to come down and do not let up until they do. MY Son's Power, Authority and HIS Name is greater than any stronghold that is coming against you.

Now learn how to use it and speak it out of your mouth.

MY Prophets will teach you and tell you what to say. Have Mustard Seed Faith and fight the good of faith.

When the shaking comes, remember to walk in love, be quick to forgive and turn the other cheek.

Now enjoy your day and remember I love you.

~ABBA Father

MY MONEY WILL RETURN THE MOST VALUE!

OCTOBER 11, 2024

Your money situation is going to change. I have told you that Nesara is real. I have told you that silver will explode. It is finally above $30 which was the marker. Just wait, MY Children. Some of you are being impatient and blaming MY Prophets for things that I have told you that will come to pass. Wait and see.

Silver will rise quicker than gold. Did you get your silver yet?

The Iraqi Dinar and the Vietnamese Dong are the ones to look at now. The window is closing, and you need to be getting your currencies. These will rise the highest of all the currencies and you will be pleased beyond belief. Get your investments now if you can.

XRP will increase but I have told you the silver and the gold are mine and the cattle on a thousand hills. Invest in XRP if you like, but MY money will return you the most value.

The dollar is shaky, but I will straighten it out in the days to come. Don't worry MY Children as I will always take care of you. Remember the Great Wealth Transfer is right here. Soon you will see. I will be using silver, gold and world currencies as one way to prosper MY Children. But I AM the Great I AM, and I can bring you wealth so many ways. Fear not. Walk by faith. Walk by faith and keep your eyes and your heart on MY Son.

All of this will happen soon and it is for MY Son's Glory and to bring the lost home to ME. Remember I trust you MY Children, when I bring wealth to your storehouses, remember the Lord Your God. Forget not MY Son and Our Covenant with you. Do not be distracted by the sudden change in your wallet. Stay humble and do not be arrogant.

Now what are you doing today? Pause a time or two and talk to me.

I love you,

ABBA Father

NOVEMBER 5TH WILL BE A GREAT DAY!
OCTOBER 15, 2024

Let MY Son be Lord and King in your life. You call Him the King of Kings and the Lord of Lords, but is He really on the day-to-day? Seek Him and get to know Him in a more personal way. He is the most exciting person to ever live. He came as a Lamb and has the boldness of a Lion. He healed the sick, raised the dead and calmed the storms. Let Him calm the storms in your life.

He is the Prince of Peace and He will give you peace beyond understanding. No matter what you are walking through. He paid the ultimate price for you to be healed, fully restored and have eternal life with ME in heaven.

Choose wisely MY children as you do not know the hour or day that you will be gone, and your choice will be made.

So, you are here to hear MY Voice. I love that you are desiring to know MY Heart and MY Words to MY Prophets. There will be much to tell you in the days to come; but, for now, you are in the waiting period. Waiting on the election and waiting on ME to move in this earth.

The election is very soon and MY Movement in this earth is very soon. Be patient MY Little Ones and soon you will see all. You will dance and celebrate and eat your cake. Be ready.

Trump has said November 5th will be the best day. It will be a great day! Make sure you vote as it is important to vote and exercise your freedom as a US citizen. Vote early if you can and you will celebrate. I have told you Trump/Vance and Trump/Vance it will be.

There will be no steal as MY Church has finally woken up. Pray for the safe, secure election and safety for voters as they go to the polls.

This election is about your freedom and freedom you shall have and keep as it is not the devil's time yet.

Let freedom reign in MY beautiful United States. The land of the free and the home of the brave. Let freedom ring!

All of this is for the Glory of MY Dear Son and to bring in the Final Great Harvest of Souls. It is all coming together and soon you will see.

Now go and rest and play and get your work done. But don't forget ME and MY Son.

Love,

ABBA Father

CRYPTO & A RED TIDE

OCTOBER 17, 2024

I AM the Great I AM, and I AM Merciful and Kind; I AM Love and I extend MY Goodness to all MY Children. Receive MY Love and let ME fill your life with MY Goodness.

Get the idols out of your life. You say, what idols? I am not bowing down to other gods such as wood, stone, Budda or Mohammad. O, but many of you are. You worship celebrities, sports, your TV shows, people in your life, your home and even yourself. Come to ME and repent and let ME help you with all of that. I AM Merciful and I can help you change your heart and turn away from idolatry of things and people to a right relationship with all of that. Bow down and worship ME and MY Son only. Put US first and foremost in your life and you will find more peace, more fullness and more understanding in your life. You will have more joy. You will not have to eliminate things you enjoy but repent from making them most the most important.

As for money, MY Word says the love of money is the root of all evil. You need money and you must have it to function. But you are not to worship it or be in love with your money or how much you crave or desire. Put ME and MY Son first in your life and get on MY Methods of giving, sowing and reaping and you will have more than enough to fulfill the desire of your heart.

Crypto currency is a way that I will prosper. It is not MY Created money – gold, silver, and MY Metals will exceed the increase of crypto. Invest wisely MY Children as I give you direction. Look for currencies that are based on MY Gold. The gold and the silver is MINE and the cattle on a thousand hills.

The time has come for the world to know that I AM the Great I AM. MY display of justice, truth and righteousness is beginning to pour out. The evil ones cannot fake the truth any longer.

Expect a red tide. Many will change their hearts of stone at the last moment as they will know the truth and the truth will set them free.

Audra, you are MY Faithful Girl, and I AM very proud of you. Your rest is coming soon. BE faithful and stay close to ME and I will give you the energy, strength, wisdom and balance that you need until May. Then you will reap your reward and your heart's desire.

Wake up, MY Children and walk in love today and each day. Be kind and let your light shine. Let MY Son's love flow through you and let others see Him through you.

Be anxious, not for tomorrow or any day thereafter. Enjoy this day! As this is the day that I have made.

Love,

ABBA Father

SNUB OF THE CATHOLIC DINNER, TRUMP & A TIDAL WAVE
OCTOBER 18, 2024

MY Son is all powerful and all wonderful. He paid the price for you and all of you. WE will never leave you nor forsake you and everything is under control. It is all falling into place and WE are in control.

The snub of the Catholic dinner in New York on Thursday is the first of many blunders you will see in the coming days as we lead up to a great day. A day that will begin the restoration of the United States back to the land of the free and the home of the brave. A day that will begin a period of prosperity like no other. A day that will begin MY young people being set free from a woke agenda of brainwashing them into confusion, sex change and other crazy nonsense straight from the pit of hell.

Trump is returning but you are called to do your part. Your part is to vote and to help if you can. Your part is to pray and not sit idly by expecting it to happen without you involved.

Pray for the election. Pray for Trump and Vance and their families. Pray for the safety of the polls and the voters. Pray and be vigilant. Do not go to sleep or let your lamp go out now. Trump is not your Bridegroom or a Savior. He is a man that I picked to lead the country for such a time as this. He is a flawed man just as all of you are. But he loves MY Son and is not afraid to admit it and he loves the USA and the people of this country.

Pray for his Presidency and the people he surrounds himself with. Pray for the election of the Senate and the House. Now is not the enemy's time and it is MY choice and not theirs as to who will lead this country and how long she (the USA) will stand. But MY children that is not a worry for today. Today, prepare for your future. The greatest and most exciting time in history.

The tide is coming, and it will be a tidal wave. Stay up and watch and celebrate. There will be no steal and there are not enough illegal imported voters. I AM the Great I AM, and you are going to be amazed.

Now take a moment and love on your family. Call a friend and pause in your day. Try not to be so busy.

We love you so much.

~ABBA Father

ZIMBABWE BOND & A GREAT DAY FOR THE UNITED STATES & SILVER OCTOBER 20, 2024

Today will be a great day for the United States. A day like no other. This day will bring the greatest change the world has seen in modern times. You will cheer and celebrate, high-five and dance. Celebrate MY Children as this is the time you have prayed and hoped for.

So now what? There is massive cleanup and rebuilding in the country. Your continual President, Commander-in-Chief, will lead the charge and you will be proud of your country again. The streets will clean up and safety will rise. Health will increase as Big Pharma, Medical fraud and insurance are exposed. The industry will change and health will be restored to this land for a while. Be ready, MY Children – this great day is upon you.

Nelson Chamisa will be elected and installed as the leader of Zimbabwe. The currency will flourish. The Zimbabwe bond will exceed all of the currencies in growth. It is the one to buy and invest in now. The door is closing as the election will be soon and that will be the trigger of the increase.

Look at Silver – I have told of the increase. It has increased and is going up, but, Oh, it will explode. I have told you.

So be ready as all will come to pass of MY Words.

MY Word and MY Love never fail. Get to know MY Precious Son Jesus. He will change your life (Alleluia). He made the way for you. He paid the price, and He did the hardest, worst part for you to know ME. Come to US today. Carolyn will tell you how.

How you said your prayers today? Give US a few minutes of your time and bring your problems, your dreams, your desires to US. WE are the dream makers, promise keepers, problem solvers and WE will give you peace and joy in the midst of the worst storm of your life. Just cry out to ME and MY Son. WE love you so much. WE long for you to come to US, but WE gave you freewill and it is your call when, how and how much time you will give to US. WE are always here no matter where you are.

Go out today and enjoy time with the people in your life. Ask ME to help you with those that are not easy for you to deal with. MY Son is the Prince of Peace and you can have His Peace no matter what.

WE love you with an everlasting heart.

~ABBA Father

HARRIS TO COLLAPSE IN POLLS
& A NIGHTMARE IN THE LIBERAL CAMP

OCTOBER 21, 2024

Put your faith in MY Son – the one Who will never leave nor forsake you. The Bridegroom that you have confidence in will always take care of you. The Friend that is always there for you and laid down His life for you. Remember Him and trust in Him.

Start your day with ME and MY Son. Let US fill you fresh before you turn on your television. WE can give you peace and joy despite what the world is telling you.

There are two things that are getting ready to happen. You will know them when you see them. These two things will push Harris/Waltz further down in the polls and booster President Trump up further. Expect Harris to collapse in the polls and it will be a nightmare in the liberal camp. Pray for her and all their souls again. I do not want them to perish but they have chosen the evil one and are pushing his agenda.

Did you vote yet? The lines are long because MY Church has woken up. It is about time, but you are right on time. You needed to see this evil at this level for ME to be able to stop it. MY Methods and Ways are not yours. I AM the Great I AM, and I know best. I have all wisdom, and I AM Love. I love all of MY Creation, and it grieves ME that some will not accept ME and MY Son. It is a free choice that I gave as you want people to freely choose to love you and not be forced. WE feel the same way. Pray for the evil ones again that they repent and turn from their evil ways and receive ME and MY Son Jesus. Jesus is the only Way to ME. MY Son, Yeshua, is the Way, the Truth and the Life. Receive Him today and make Him the Lord of your life.

Your money and finances are changing. Your life is changing. Your family is changing, and you are going to have the greatest days of your life. Stay close to ME and MY Son and let US love on you today.

Love,

ABBA Father

HOW DARE KAMALA!

OCTOBER 23, 2024

This is the season that you have long awaited and longed for. It is here. They will soon be gone – the evil ones. You see it coming now. The stress and fatigue and failure is starting to weigh on the deep state. Watch them crumble and fall apart over the next couple of weeks.

Pray for the safety of Trump/Vance and their families. There is evil on the loose, but I will protect them. I give MY Angel Armies to watch over them.

Did you know that Kamala is lying more and more? It saddens ME that she has gone this far in her path to rule the US.

But you MY Church must do you part. Pray and vote! Pray and vote! Do not assume you are not needed on either level. The Body of Christ, I call you to pray and vote. Vote early if you can. This is the most important election of your lifetime. Do not sit idly by and let others make your choice. Do your part. I want back in MY Government. I want back in MY schools. I want back in America. MY land founded on MY Book – The Holy Bible. MY Book does not say anything about a separation of church and state. MY (good) Kings of Israel had a Priest by their side and sought their advice. My good

Kings of Israel sought the priests to advise them based on MY Law – not man-made law. MY good Kings took the wise advice of the priests that I put before them.

How dare Kamala not recognize MY Son at her rally and shamed MY young men who stood up for Jesus. Her polls will plummet and her words will haunt her when she finishes the race. She will regret her words and know that she has picked the wrong side. Kamala, turn before it is too late.

Today is a great day and you should rest and play. Come to spend time with ME and love one another.

We love you.

WAKE UP MY CHURCH!

OCTOBER 27, 2024

This is going to be a great week. Trump will continue to surge and soar and the Harris/Waltz crowd will plummet.

Trolling at churches will not work. Faking as a preacher will not work. Denying MY Son and using His Church does not mix.

Wake up MY Church and do not be deceived by their evil rhetoric. They are grasping for straws and will jump on any bandwagon or policy that might grab a select group. They are decided and will be dismayed at the display of truth, justice and righteousness that will reign in the land.

I win and you win. The battle has been very fierce and the fiery darts will continue, but you MY Precious loved ones must do your part. Do not let up. Pray and vote. Now if you have not done so yet.

MY David, that I picked before he was knitted together in his mother's womb is making ME very proud. He has stood tall and is fighting the good fight of faith. I will not let you or him down. With MY Hand, he will make American great again and the country will stand. This hatred and unrest will cease and there will be joy in the streets.

You can count on ME and MY Son. WE are restoring America and getting rid of the evil ones to usher in the great wealth transfer and final multi-billion soul harvest.

MY Son's Bride will preach and teach the Gospel throughout the world and MY Precious children will use the wealth to ensure MY Son's Gospel is fully funded.

There is no one like MY Beautiful, Precious Son, Jesus. Give HIM your life now. Do not miss the wonderful life WE have reserved just for you. A life of joy, peace, contentment, prosperity and hope. Call on HIM now. HE will receive you no matter where you are, what path you have chosen or how you look. WE love you. WE care about you. But you must choose US as WE will never force ourselves on you.

Now look up, your redemption is near for all that you need.

I love you,

ABBA Father

CHAOS & STRIFE IN THEIR CAMP!!!

CELEBRATE! CELEBRATE!

OCTOBER 28, 2024

There is a difference between what you see and what is happening. You see the Democrats pushing their agenda – acting all puffed up and confident; but they are not. There is chaos and strife in their camp and fear on top. Fear is spreading throughout the Democratic Party. The kind of fear that can be paralyzing.

Be ready to celebrate. There are more on MY Side than theirs. Remember this is a battle for good and evil. This battle is to save the United States from the pit of hell. This battle is a choice between ME, the Great God Jehovah or satan. Who do you choose to serve today? Choose ME, the Great I AM. Vote MY Bible. MY Holy Love Book. Vote for the future of your children. Vote to save the USA which will save the world. Do not be lazy or complacent. Vote like your vote will determine the outcome of the race for the President.

Remember I will move, but I often work through you MY Children. At this time, today your part is to vote. Now do your part and continue to pray.

Then after the election, I want MY Church to continue to be on your knees praying.

I AM the Great I AM and soon you will be amazed at the signs and wonders I will display and allow to happen. It is a glorious time. Celebrate! Celebrate!! Dance to the music (3 Dog night playing in my head).

Put your rapture rug away for a season as you do your Christmas decorations. MY Son is coming soon, but there is a glorious season upon you before He comes for His Bride. So, enjoy the beautiful, glorious time and prepare to be the beautiful Bride of MY Son Jesus the Christ. Give Him all the praise and glory.

This time is a time when the greatest soul harvest will occur and the world will change for a good season of time. Read MY Word, spend time with US and invite the Holy Spirit to lead you every day.

Give US some time and let the light of My Son shine. Do not dim or cover up your light that MY Son has put in you. Walk gently and carry a big stick for MY Son. These are great days and the harvest is ready. Be a harvester of souls for MY Son. Be a harvester of souls to change people's lives. Be a harvester of souls to lay up treasure in heaven where rust and moth will never steal your precious treasures.

Come and drink from the fruit of the Vine of MY Son and experience a more wonderful life with US.

WE love you,

ABBA Father

GO IN FAITH TODAY!

MAKE A DIFFERENCE IN THE LIVES OF PEOPLE!

OCTOBER 31, 2024

You are going to be amazed and in awe very, very soon. This does not mean that the enemy will stop their attack, but as MY Glory fills the whole earth, you will experience a new level of miracles, signs, wonders, health and prosperity. This is for you, MY Children, because WE love you. It is the time for you to be set free. I AM not setting you free because of a man named Trump. I am setting you free because of MY Son, Jesus, who came in the form of a man. HE is MY Son and I AM so proud of Him. I AM setting you free because I love you and I want MY children to have the freedom that MY Precious Son bought and paid for by going to the cross, dying and being resurrected on the third day. Give MY Son the Glory and do not be ashamed to tell all about MY Precious Son. He will never leave you nor forsake you. The days to come will have their events and it will be interesting, shocking and a time of glory – The glory is coming and soon you will feel it. Seek the Glory – Call it in. Declare it over your household. Declare it over your family. Expect it and believe for it.

215

Do you have a testimony of what WE have done for you? Share it. Tell somebody. That one you tell may need to know. Your testimonies give people hope. Remind them that MY Son can do this and more for them. WE are no respecters of persons and WE will answer all prayers. All prayers will be answered. Some will come in ways that you want and desire. Some will come answered differently. Our ways are not your ways. But Our ways are always the best. Trust ME.

Great is your reward for having faith. We put it in you. Now use it. Ask US to develop your faith to be bold like MY Son. You only need a mustard seed of faith for US to move in your life. Speak to the mountains in front of you and command them to go and use MY Son Jesus' name. He gave you His Authority.

WE have given you all of the tools that you need to be victorious in every area of your life.

Now go in faith today and make a difference in the lives of the people in your life. Be the light that He has put in you when you received MY Precious Son, Yeshua as Lord and Savior.

We love you with an everlasting heart.

~ABBA Father

THE PUZZLE YOU HAVE BEEN
TRYING TO PUT TOGETHER
NOVEMBER 1, 2024

You think you know what is happening, but it is not all as it seems. I have given you valuable jagged puzzle pieces, but you have not fit them together correctly. Your puzzle pieces are not fitting into the correct slots. Hold on, I will rearrange the puzzle pieces for you. Some of you see how I have placed and fitted them all together. It will be amazingly, wonderful in a way that you have never dreamed. I do not need an election to change the world. I only need one day and the day is upon you. MY Prophets are all speaking to you of this day and they all prophecy today and this is sent to give you a message of hope, love and that your future is bright. (you need to wear shades).

Glory days are upon you. I AM Love and I love all of you MY Precious Children. I send you these messages. I want you not listening to each other; just ME.

Go be in your prayer closet and be excited and ready to celebrate. MY Prophets of old often brought gloom and doom messages to the King and the children of Israel; but MY new prophets bring a message of love and hope because I want you to put down all worry, anxiety and fear. But you say, I can't. Speak out loud. In the name of Jesus, fear you must go. Every knee must bow, and every tongue confess that MY Son Jesus is Lord. Open your hearts to Him today. He will change your life (alleluia, amen, amen).

Fear not the days ahead. I have told you Trump/Vance will lead the country. Fear not. Everything is changing now. Miracles are breaking out. I AM on the throne, and it is well.

Love,

ABBA Father

A FEARFUL DREAM AND
THE MILITARY WILL HAVE TO COME OUT!
NOVEMBER 3, 2024

The Dream

I dreamed I was in a detention facility wearing a blue dress – prison material. The government was detaining me for Jesus. Then someone came and a lady took me to another building. Before we walked in they said: there will be two men doing something on a table. We don't know what that is. Just don't pay any attention to it. There were two men on a table, and they looked like they were wrestlers and we walked on past them. Then I was in a room with a bed and maybe sleeping. I was still at the detention or prison, and I knew they were saving me from the worst part of the prison and hiding me. A lady came in wearing fuchsia pants and a white top. She was there to help me and brought me something different to wear. Perhaps to be classified in a certain way. When we had walked past the two men on the table, the lady and I went into a room with more ladies, and they were happy for me to be there and they would help me.

NOVEMBER 3, 2024

You have nothing to fear; I AM always with you even to the ends of the earth. That dream was not from ME. I will not allow it to happen to you. Rest in ME. You will live out your days with your family and I have promised that I will take care of you, Daniel, Michael and Brinkley. I will not take you from your family until you all come home together and that will be when MY Son comes to get you. So forget that and fear not.

The election will be red across the board. Fear not.

Every office in the land is going red and the evil ones will be gone. I have said it. The military will have to come out now as Pelosi and the others are in great fear and will fight to avoid their treason charges. But the charges are coming. The nation has already decided and the vote on Tuesday will be massive for Trump. Now rest on what I have told you MY Girl and don't apologize or back down. Your faith has been strong. Fast on Tuesday.

I love you,

ABBA Father

RED SURGE ACROSS THE LAND!

NOVEMBER 4, 2024

This season that you have been through has come and is almost gone. Yes, there will be repercussions from the Red Surge across the land. But I will deal with each one and they will fade away as do all of the works of man. Now it is time for the party – time to celebrate and give thanks. Remember Me and MY Son in all of your joyous celebration. Praise and take time to give thanks to ME and MY Son. We have brought you through it all. We held back many of the plans that the enemy had for you. Look at what they have done to MY J'6ers. They had worse plans for many of you; but WE held them back.

The J'6ers will be set free and I will repair the collateral damage in their lives.

Woe to the ones who brought about all of this debacle. Woe to the ones who sat and schemed to ruin people's lives because of their fear of their crimes. Repent, repent now.

Much has been done by a select few who wielded their power around like kings or mini gods. You are neither. I AM the Great I AM, and I say repent for everything that you have brought on this country and all of the lives you have taken and ruined for your greed, your fortune, your fame and for being important. Has the world stage been worth it? You will have treason on you, and you <u>are</u> going to pay the just penalty for treason against the people of the United States of America. Did you really think you were above the law and that you could steal MY United States?

Kamala, Kamala, it is time to shut up and stop laughing. MY United States is not yours for the taking. This is MY land, and I say who rules and I decide the ruler. You, Kamala have broken more that I will name and Nancy, too. You all should repent now as your time is up and soon all will know how bad you have used and abused the power and trust given to you in this land that I love.

America, America, you are once again free. Be free now and plan your freedom celebration.

Now go and have a great day!

I love you,

ABBA Father

THE GREAT HEALTH TRANSFER

NOVEMBER 9, 2024

I AM going to use Robert Kennedy as a vessel to set the country free from sickness and disease. He will on Day 1 make major changes in the food and drug industry that will help you. MY People are perishing for a lack of knowledge. Wake up Church and smell the coffee. Coffee is one, but it is everything in your pantry and your medicine cabinet and on your nightstand.

Get ready for the Body of Christ to slim down and the obesity problem in this country to dissolve. Get ready MY Church for your bodies to begin to heal themselves as I designed them to do so. Get ready Church for long life, renewed hope and energy and emotional and mental health issues to straighten out. This program implemented by Bobby Kennedy will dramatically change the health and well-being of America.

I have told you there will be Glory Days. Glory Days include your health and not just your wallet. As the changes are implemented by Kennedy and team, America will flourish.

No longer will the evil ones be putting toxins into your food. No longer will the evil ones be pushing their poisonous vaccines on MY People.

223

Be open and ready for the changes that are coming to MY Body in your physical body. Miracles will seem to occur with people as these changes are implemented. But much will be MY People gaining wisdom and making changes in their health due to their lifestyle changes.

Your body is MY Temple, and I want you healthy – mentally, physically and emotionally. I have great plans for MY Body, and I need a Church that is whole and healthy. I need a Church that is energized and ready to complete the Great Commission of My Precious Son, Jesus.

I have told you of the Great Wealth Transfer. It is also time for the Great Health Transfer as changes are implemented in the US Food and Drug Administration. Listen carefully to MY son, Bobby Kennedy. He belongs to ME, and I AM using him for MY Glory.

Bobby is a very wise man and WE have made the way for him to Make America Healthy Again. So look up MY Church; your redemption draw near.

America will be free and healthy. These are Glory Days! They are here. Get ready, everything is changing now.

I love you,

ABBA Father

A LOVE LETTER TO YOU FROM GOD!

NOVEMBER 12, 2024

I love you with an everlasting heart and that will never change. MY Love for you is more than you can ask or think. I have dreams and visions for you. So dream bigger. Write it down and plan larger. Write down your dreams and desires for you and your family. Speak out what you desire and start dreaming and declaring it. I told you in MY Holy Bible, MY Love Book, to choose life and not death. I told you to decree and declare a thing. Check MY Book. It is there. I AM not a man that I would lie. I have great plans for you. Dream it, ask for it, write the vision down, and start confessing with your mouth.

Your days will be sweeter and more full of joy and peace. The things of this world will mean less and MY People will mean more . You will grow to love those who are hard to love and you will grow in your walk to become more like MY Son, Yeshua. Praise His Name forever.

So, MY Dear Child, this message is for you and for your family. Take hold of MY Words and listen carefully. I have given this word for you to sing and dance and to grow closer to ME.

I love you so much. As you grow and follow MY Pathways, I can bless you more and more. The blessings you desire may change over time; but, they will be richer and more meaningful.

I love you so much!

~ABBA Father

SEVEN YEARS OF GLORY! YOUR VATS & STOREHOUSES WILL BE FULL & OVERFLOW!

NOVEMBER 14, 2024

Seven years of Glory. The Glory is manifesting on the earth, and it is going to be the most beautiful, glorious time for MY Precious Children. Get ready to have provision and harvest like you never dreamed. Get ready, MY Bride, to see the fullness of the prophecies of MY Great Prophets. They have spoken of MY Glory and now it is time for it to manifest.

The trigger was the Trump/Vance win. Now believers and those with pure hearts are being put in place and I can move those mountains in your life. I can prosper your hand and heal your bodies. The United States has had a principality over the land since Obama took office. Roe v. Wade brought another principality. So the overturning of Roe took away the first and now the Trump victory will remove the second. These principalities have ruled over this land through the evil ones who have crammed their demonic agenda down your throats. No more until MY Church/Bride comes home to US. No more, I say and I AM dealing with these evil ones. Justice is Mine saith the Lord of Hosts and I will have MY Justice on them. Vengeance is Mine. You will hear of some of their justice and vengeance, but these are not the day matters for you.

It is between ME and them. They will face ME. Some will repent now, some later and some never. I AM Love and Merciful. I will forgive all of them that truly repent from a pure heart.

This is the time of Joseph, and I AM calling MY Josephs. You know who you are. You have been stockpiling and now is the time for you to share your wealth. Seek ME and find ME and I will direct your paths. Ask ME to dispense the wealth and I will show you the places that are fertile ground that will reap greater harvest than you ever dreamed or desired.

MY Church/Bride, it is time for you to forgive. Forgive the evil ones and those around you who do not see the light. Forgive those who have wronged you throughout your life. Come to ME, humble yourself on your knees and I will help you and heal you in the process. I cannot bless you with unforgiveness in your heart towards even the worst of the evil ones. Have pity on them and pray for them. They are lost and I want them found.

Support and cheer for the men and women that MY David is picking. The USA will be restored to the land of the free and the home of the brave. It is Glory Time.

Look for MY Glory and bask in the Glory. Wedge out time to be with ME and My Precious Son, Jesus. WE love you so much and want very much to give you the desires of your heart. WE cannot bless you to the fullest if you harbor hate, unforgiveness, haughtiness and pride. Cast them down and get up with a pure heart walking in love. The love of MY Son. Love like Him. Follow Him and master His teachings. Earn a master's degree in MY Bible. But you say, I don't want to go back to the University. No, you don't need that. Study MY Word. Read the Bible – MY Love Book. Read it a little each day. MY Word will begin to get in your heart and your life. MY Word became Flesh, and the Flesh is MY Beautiful, Precious Son Jesus. Find a Church or Fellowship. If there is not the right one in your distance, find an online one. Get in a Bible Study. MY Girls, Audra and Carolyn always have one and there are plenty online. Get involved in service to ME. Ask ME what your service area is if you do not know.

You want me to bless you? I AM. But I have asked you to be a blessing in MY Kingdom and to people. Sow your time, your gifts, your talents and yes, your money into MY Kingdom. The more you give <u>with a pure heart</u>, the more I can surprise and bless you. Ask ME for direction and I will answer you.

So rejoice. This is the time of prosperity and overflow as in the days of Joseph. Your vats and storehouses will be full and overflow. Just follow MY Plan, but I AM looking to and frow over the earth for MY People with pure hearts.

Enjoy your day and declare your destiny!

Love,

ABBA Father

THE VIEW, FAKE NEWS & KAMALA

NOVEMBER 17, 2024

Now think about where you are and where you want to be in your life. Are you there yet? If not, I can take you there and to even better. Trust in ME and just wait and see.

You have not because you ask not. Seek ME first and the Kingdom of God and you shall have more than you can ask or think. Exceedingly, abundantly above all of the rest and more. I will bless you in the city and I will bless you in the field. I can make you the head and not the tail. Walk with ME and talk to ME today. Tell ME your dreams, wants and desires. I will not disappoint you. Remember MY Son Jesus walked on the water. He performed miracles, signs and wonders and some still did not believe that He is the Christ, MY Beautiful, Precious Son.

Invite Him into your heart now. He will change your life and take away those struggles and frustrations that you are dealing with on a daily basis.

Now what about the country now that the election is over. Are you still celebrating? Remember to cheer and shout and give ME thanks as you see the next series of blunders on one side and promotions on the other. Which side do you pick today? Choose life that you may live. Choose

231

life for MY precious babies. Choose life for MY young people. Choose life for MY people.

This is a new era and a new day. January 20th will start a four-year dynasty for the United States of America. This four years will overflow into four more with good, Christian men and women at the helm.

I AM dealing with the View and the fake news and their lies and venom. Most of them were kind of nice for a day, but it is time they realize who they are – mere dust that have been overly promoted because they can speak and have confidence. I will change their hearts but first I must dismantle all of this rhetoric and shut them down. I do not need you to assist ME as I shut them down, but by not watching these lies and snake venom, you will see clearer the truth. Joy, you will have days of no joy if you continue to refuse to repent and turn from your evil ways. Choose your course now.

And what about Kamala? The American people have killed her political career. Go home Kamala. You are gone girl as I said she would be. Look in the mirror and see who you allowed yourself to become for your evil agenda and your greed of power and money. Repent, I say repent. You have already died politically, and you are close to being dead spiritually. Change your ways; talk to ME before it is too late.

So, what do you think of Trump's picks? There are the best of the best. Talented, sharp, articulate men and women, I picked them and put them all on Trump's heart. I gathered this group from all over to change the course of this nation and the course of the world. It is not the time for the evil one to take over. Of course, he is still causing problems and stirring up trouble, but this is MY time. Glory times. The time that the ancients of old wrote about and longed to see. A time made especially for you and for ME to reap the final great multi-billion soul harvest. So look up, your redemption draws neigh. It is Glory and harvest time. The time for miracles to break out in churches, in Walmart and in your home. You will see much manifestation and MY Hand is on all of it. Just sit tight. Have not I already told you so many things that you have seen come to pass. Much, much more is on the way from ME to you and yours. Just wait and see.

Today is a beautiful, great day – another gift from ME. Enjoy and love on your family.

I AM so proud of each of you. I handcrafted you and your talents and gifts.

I love you,

ABBA Father

PRODIGALS ARE COMING HOME!

HOW TO STOP SOME OF YOUR PROBLEMS!

NOVEMBER 19, 2024

You will love the next four years. They are going to be glorious and full of sweet days for MY Precious Children. It will be a time of health, prosperity, overflow and peace and joy.

As Trump and team work MY Plan, the nation will heal. A Miracle Healing for the nation of the US and the world. I AM the Great I AM and there is none like ME. I make MY Choices based on MY Plan not man's plan.

The nation will heal quickly, and MY Word will be restored in this land. Finances will be restored. Miracles will break out as MY Glory fills this earth. O' the Glory – the Glory of MY Precious Son Jesus.

There is a time and a purpose under heaven. The time and purpose for now is MY Children that have been lost and now they will be found. MY Prodigals and Wanderers are coming home. Home to ME and home to families they left over heated arguments and disagreements over lifestyles, choices and people in their lives. Healing will break out as MY Truth returns to this land and throughout the world. Health and healing to your bodies, health and healing to your family, health and healing to MY Children and young people. Health and healing to marriages, health and healing for finances, health and healing to MY Schools and the curriculum that MY Children learn. The sick, diabolical demonic woke curriculum being taught MY Children will be gone. No more, I say no more. I have had enough of men dressing up as clown looking women and influencing MY Little Children. I have had enough of MY Government and teachers encouraging MY Children to be something they are not. I created two genders – male and female and there is NO more. If this debauchery of being a they or a cat is in your home, repent for allowing it in. Find the break in what allowed it and repent to ME. Learn how to get rid of it. Get right with ME and use your spiritual authority to rid your home of the demonic. Choose Life. Do you clean your house with mops and brooms? Do you wash your body and your hair? Spiritually clean your physical house. Ask someone how to do that, who knows. You are at the right place on this channel to learn. MY Girls are teaching you. Wake up and pay attention. Use your faith and exercise the actions required to remove the evil that has seemingly innocently come into your home. Go through your belongings, look on your walls. What are you watching and what are you letting your kids watch for your convenience? Clean the house. Command the demonic to leave and cleanse your house and family members with the Precious Blood of My Beautiful Son, Yeshua. Don't wait. The enemy roams too and frow looking for whom he can kill, steal and destroy; but MY Son Jesus came that you have life and have it more abundantly.

Now get to work on making your home and your heart pure. If you are unsure of things, ask someone and first ask ME. Ask the Holy Spirit. WE will tell you. Ask US to reveal what needs to go and what needs changing in you and your life. This is all preparation for MY Glory and to protect you against the wile, evil plans of the enemy.

Now be still today and know ME. I tell you these things because I love you and I have great plans for you. Take care of it, starting now. Do not delay. This will stop some of the problems.

I love you MY Beautiful Children.

~ABBA Father (Adonai)

DO NOT FEAR NUCLEAR WAR!

GREAT CHANGE IN THE MEDIA!

NOVEMBER 19 & 20, 2024

Do not fear tomorrow or the days to come. Expect the Glory and expect great things to happen. Do not fear the threat of nuclear war or anything they say may happen if this or that happens. I AM that I AM, and I have MY Hand on it all and no weapon shall prosper which forms against you. There will be no weapons of mass destruction used at this time. The days will pass and soon it will be January 1. The excitement will continue and all will be well.

The left will proceed to nick-pick and needle, but their bitterness and tongues of fire will fade away as they slowly give up the fight. I AM moving in the hearts of many and soon you will see great change in the media.

You will see miracles, signs and wonders begin to manifest as the New Year rolls in. Roll tide! The tide has turned with the Red Tide Victory. There will be no stopping the great plans that I have for this earth and for each of you.

Today, I want you to know, if you hear nothing else, that WE love you and WE see your struggles, your worry and your pain. WE are always here. Come to US and spend some time. WE are moving in your life even when you don't see it. The best is yet to come, and it is NOW!

Wait and see.

Love,

ABBA Father

TRUMP – THE MASTER CHESS PLAYER;

THE GREAT & TERRIBLE DAY
NOVEMBER 21 & 22, 2024

You are not going to believe the checkmate that is coming. Trump has much up his sleeve, and he has been working on it for over four years. He is a Master Chess Player, and he is going to master this game of chess against the Dems and the far-left Rhinos.

Did you hear about Gaetz? This is a move on the board, and it will enhance Trump's win. There are no black diamonds in Trump's game; but the slopes will be green, and all of the pieces will fall into place. Wait and see.

There is a day coming that I have spoken of quite frequently. It is in MY Holy Bible, and I have told MY Prophets. The Great and Terrible Day of the Lord. It is coming and this generation in this time are going to experience and live through it. That day everything will change. You thought that election would change everything. You think Inauguration Day will change everything. These are days of men and women – a dramatic, much needed change for a nation and the world. Woe, the Great and Terrible Day of the Lord is going to shake the world. It will not be the shaking that you normally think of. This Great and Terrible Day will shake people to their core and bring many to their knees. But do

239

not fear MY Precious Child. This day will bring the freedom that I want you all to have. Markets will crash and there will be fires. Fires of destruction and fires of purification. Fires that cleanse from the inside out. As a forest fire brings new, beautiful growth in a short amount of time, fire refines the gold that you wear and the gold you desire. Fire that will change and purify the hearts of many and usher in MY multi-billion soul harvest. (I hear your prayers, Steve). Fire that will change MY World and to usher in the Greater Glory. Prepare for this Great and Terrible Day through praise of MY Precious Son Yeshua. Praise Him in the morning and all throughout your day. Seek Him and think of Him and be sure to tell all about Him as you go along your way. Press in and give US an extra minute or two of your time. Prepare for this Great and Terrible Day by reading MY Word – MY Love Book, The Holy Bible. Prepare by forgiving your neighbor and all you are offended by and even forgiving yourself. Prepare by not fretting or worrying. It will be a one-day event and I only need one day to change the world and the world will change and when you see your new world, you will rejoice and be glad.

So, take a moment. Give thanks today that you are MINE. Remember I love you and it will all be well.

Love,

ABBA Father

MONEY & THE GREAT DAY

NOVEMBER 22 & 24, 2024

My Bright and Morning Star shall rule and reign forevermore. He is MY Son – the Rock of All Ages. He will never leave you nor forsake you and He laid down His life that you might have life and have it more abundantly. Stay close to ME now as the days are getting shorter to the Great and Terrible Day of the Lord. I AM warning the Bride of MY Dear Son to not let your lamps go out nor fall asleep on the watch. Be vigilant in your prayers and while you wait. The Election, the Inauguration and MY Great Day are all tied together, but you must just wait and see. I told you what will happen and it is quite obvious, but you are blinded by the way man would do it. I AM the Great I AM and there is no one like ME. I can change the times and I change the seasons. There is no one like ME and there never will be. Trust ME that you have no need to fret, worry or to be in fear. I want you on your watch and at your post. You know your spot and for MY Prayer Warriors do not let up. You are on a stealth mission, and you will be greatly rewarded. Now stand firm.

Take some time each day to pray to ME. Tell ME your dreams, your desires and your needs and your wants. Praise MY Son and as you praise you open the heavens and MY Glory shall fill the earth.

You are in a waiting time – like standing in a line. You can choose to get upset, fret and worry, be impatient or be at peace. The Great Shaking is coming, and I warn you because I love you. But I tell you again to fear not.

You ask MY Prophet about the money. Fear not whether the money will do this or that. I AM the Great I AM and all that I have told you will come to pass. MY Gold and MY Silver will do the best and it will happen. You are still in the holding pattern and it is the time to wait and fix your thoughts on other things. So make your investments, buy your currencies and put them away. Don't go look at them or count them. That is for another day in the future very soon. Just fix your thoughts on MY Son and your mission for His Kingdom. Assess your heart. Are you Kingdom-minded for yourself or for MY Son? Be like MY Girl Audra and be Kingdom-minded for MY Dear Son Yeshua. There are people around you who need you to tell them about Yeshua and you are the one they will hear and make an impact in their life.

No go frolic and play. Enjoy this day. Catch MY Glorious sunset if you can. Admire MY Stars and smell MY Flowers. All created for specific purpose and for you to enjoy.

I love you always,

ABBA Father

TIME AND MONEY

NOVEMBER 26, 2024

This is the time for all of MY People to come to the table and show the love of MY Dear Son, Yeshua to one and all. There seems to be so much hate, but there is much love in MY Beautiful World. Start sharing MY Son's love on your daily walk. Show His Love on your drive and give people a break. Stop yelling at distracted drivers and do not use your hand signals.

But first, you must show MY Son's Love in your home. Look at the beautiful people in your life. You all were hand-picked to be together as families. Learn to love each other and show the love of MY Dear Son. Take a moment and think about the good qualities of each of your loved ones. Take time to appreciate them and don't forget to tell them that you love them. Everyone wants to hear it, including ME.

Give your family a break on the little things that irritate you that are of no consequence. And let them have their way from time to time.

Come sit with ME and let ME speak directly to you. I want you to know ME much better and I have secrets I want to share with only you.

243

MY Prophets hear MY Voice, but you can too, and I have put MYSELF in each of you. Be still and know ME.

Take your time to grow in ME and with your family. Your life is but a vapor in the window of time and you don't want to miss the time that you have because when it is gone, it is gone, and you cannot go back.

Your time is much more valuable than your money. Money can come and money can go; but your time comes and then it is gone. What are you doing with your life that will be everlasting in MY Kingdom? Loving on people is the most important thing you can do for ME. Show love and love like ME and MY Son. Let your life be a demonstration of MY love for them.

We need harvesters to bring in the multi-billion soul harvest that is coming very soon. A bumper crop and they will be ripe for the picking. Remember if you do all kinds of works for ME and MY Son and you don't do them in love, it is for nothing.

Look today and see MY Goodness in this earth and love one another.

With love,

Adonai

DONKEYS, BATHROOMS & DEI

NOVEMBER 27, 2024

You should watch what you are doing and wasting your time on. These are days that you should enjoy with your family and friends getting ready to celebrate MY Son's birthday. Make it His Day as you prepare for your celebration and take time here and there to remember why you are doing all of this.

Decorate your tree in honor of MY Son. He deserves the praise. Make MY Son the focus of your giving. Give and give with a pure heart. Give and ask US what are the best gifts for each person. Give and remember all of the gifts that MY Son bought and paid for you to have. And don't stress over this or that. Prepare with peace and joy and above all love.

Is it not funny how the dust is starting to settle, and it will continue as Trump gets closer to moving back in the White House. The donkeys will continue to kick up heels; but, they really have nothing to kick about. Bathrooms will return to normal; DEI will be a bad memory, and the evil agenda will back down. The donkeys will tire of their jumping around and the old donkeys will retire.

245

It is going to be a kick the donkey's behind very soon and soon you will see. The celebration will keep on and on.

Team Trump are already working and they are not even on the payroll. WE will lead and guide them to restore MY USA and MY World to MY Wonderful World. (heard what a wonderful world playing in my head).

Now go get ready for Jesus' birthday. Prepare some each day!

We celebrate in heaven too! MY Beautiful Precious Son deserves all of the praise.

Love,

Adonai

2024 WILL CLOSE AS ONE OF THE BEST

DECEMBER 1, 2024

Spend this season celebrating with family and friends the birth and resurrection of MY Precious Beautiful Son Yeshua. He deserves all of the praise. 2024 has been a turbulent year; but the year will close as one of the best. The country will rise again as the greatest and the strongest in the world. This weak demonic regime are on their way out and soon you will see, feel and taste the great changes in the USA and it will go around the world.

Do you have a family member that is purposely distant and will not communicate with you? Pray for them. The enemy has worked night and day to destroy families. Many of you have a broken relationship in your family. I love you and I AM going to restore and repair the broken in your life. Bring it to ME. Talk to ME about what happened and with whom. Did you cause it? Try to make amends if you can. Did they cause it? Forgive them and tell them if you can. I AM the Great I AM, and I AM healing and restoring families. I AM Love and I created families. MY Son paid the price for your family and to be whole and restored. Forgive, pray and walk in love and watch ME and wait on ME. I AM a Promise Keeper, and these are Glory Days, and I AM preparing MY Son's Bride for the Glorious Bridegroom.

247

Remember to be very grateful this season for the big and the small that others do for you. There are so many of MY Children in the world without. Give and give more. Ask ME how and where you should give. Give in secret and let ME bless you more. Give without expecting anything in return including a receipt or even a thank you. Give and sow into MY Son's Kingdom with a heart for the lost, the broken and the downtrodden. Let ME multiply your giving and watch what I do in this earth. It is Glory Time and it is going to be glorious and then MY Son will come for His Bride. Do you know MY Son? Make Him your Savior today. Do not delay. WE love you and want to give you your very best life.

Now look up; your redemption draws neigh.

I love you,

ABBA Father

JOE USED HUNTER TO TAKE THE FALL

DECEMBER 2, 2024

You have not because you have asked not. Seek, knock and you shall find. Seek MY Son and knock on the door and you will find Him. Receive MY Son and receive life. Life worth living. A life full of love, peace, joy and much more. You will be amazed at how WE can change your life into one you enjoy and love living.

Make today count. Spend time with ME and MY Son Jesus. Ask the Holy Spirit to manage your day and see how much better it all goes for you.

What do you need and what do you want? Have you asked ME for both? Come to ME and tell ME what you need and tell ME what you want. I AM the Provider and Supplier of your needs, wants and desires. Make ME the first one you speak to about what is going on in your life.

It's Christmas and I want you to take time to reflect on the true meaning of Christmas. Remember you are celebrating MY Son's birthday. Not yours or the other people in your life. Celebrate MY Son, the people in your life and enjoy all of the preparations and the festivities.

Were you surprised Joe pardoned Hunter? The Hunter became the hunted and this is how Hunter will be remembered. Joe used Hunter for taking the fall for all of his crimes. Stay tuned.

Now take time today to love on the people in your life and remember MY Son.

I love you,

Adonai

TRUMP, TARIFFS & CONFIRMATIONS

DECEMBER 3, 2024

I have great news for you and your family. The coming year will be more than you have asked for. You have weathered the storms that did not let up for over four years. The storm has passed, and the new day is dawning. A dawn that you have never seen or dreamed about.

MY Glory shall fill this earth and the gloom and doom, and darkness will fade away. There will be dancing and cheering in the streets as MY surprises unfold. I have placed matters on Trump's heart that will dramatically affect you and your pocketbook.

The losses you have incurred and the money you have lost (lost jobs, lost ones, lost retirement and much more) are going to return 7-fold to MY Beautiful Precious children (music in my head – ding, dong – the witch is dead, which ole witch the wicked witch).

Watch what Trump does on tariffs. The tariff move will affect you in a great way. Your bottom line will be much higher and when you give Trump the credit, remember to give ME the praise. It is all in MY Plan and I have much more for you, MY Precious Child.

Watch the confirmations as the ones Trump wants sail through. There has been much strategic planning and on Day 1 the Trump team will be the cabinet of his choice. Chess moves are being played.

Now get to your day and take a break with ME. I love you so much. There is nothing that can separate ME from you.

~ABBA Father

PS I love that you want to hear what is on MY Heart!

WAKE UP! DO YOU NEED A MEETING?

DECEMBER 6, 2024

Wake up! Wake up! Wake up! What time is it and where are we on the clock of time? Are you paying attention to what the world is doing or are you focused on your mission for MY Son, Yeshua, the King of Kings and the Lord of Lords?

What are you doing? Are you busy trying to please people for Christmas or are you thinking of MY Son coming as a Babe wrapped in swaddling clothes lying in a manger – Who is the Savior of the earth.

What are you doing? Worrying about your Christmas decorations and how much you should spend on people, so your gift looks right.

Stop all of the nonsense. Take time and pause. Look at MY Son and remember why you are here and what you are doing.

I love your celebrations, and I love that you do all of these things at Christmas. Remember they are all for nothing if they are not done with a pure heart. Decorate to celebrate MY Son's birth, not to impress your neighbors. Give to celebrate Jesus as I gave MY Son to the World as your Savior. Give with a pure heart and out of love.

Do all of your wonderful Christmas celebrations with a pure heart and out of love. If it is to impress someone else, then stop. Perhaps you and I need a little meeting. Please come see and let ME help you get your heart right. I want you to walk in love. Be like MY Son Yeshua. Every step He took on this earth and in heaven, is with love. I AM Love and Jesus is Love. WE are Love and WE love you. Strive to be more like US. WE will help you. Come, sit down, bow down if you can and let US clean out what needs to go on the inside and fill you with US. As your love grows and you become more like US, the things of this earth will grow strangely dim and what was important will not be and your heart will be on the things that matter most. MY two greatest commandments are to Love Your God with all of your heart, soul and mind and the second is like this: Love your neighbor as yourself. Be like ME and Jesus – LOVE. Ask US to help you.

If all you came for today is some dirt on someone or money matters, then please have a meeting with ME at once. I love you.

~Adonai

2025 – THE GREATEST YEAR YET! WEALTH, INVESTMENTS & THE GLORY!

DECEMBER 7, 2024

Why are you standing still and not looking up and to the future? (music playing in my head – the future is bright – you need to wear shades).

2025 is going to be the greatest year of your life yet. The Greater Glory is coming. Trump will be President again and soon you will see prices go down and pocketbooks get heavy. Heavy with income, wages, overflow, wealth transfer and inheritances. Money you have invested in will finally soar. The pieces are in place and now it is time. Remember the Israelites had seven years of plenty and 400 years later they left with overflowing hands. Wealth, they had plundered from their slave owners. Your wealth will be plundered from your slave owners and 7 years of plenty to follow.

Who are your slave owners? The government, your bills, your mortgage, your credit cards, your debt and your boss and much more.

I AM the Great I AM, and I AM setting you free. MY Precious Children will have no lack, no poverty and you will be set free. Free indeed. Wait and see!

Go to your bank accounts and all of your debt. Write it down today and put away. Come back in a few months and see if it is better. Better and better and better and better.

I have promised and it is done! I AM a Promise Keeper, and I AM not a man that would lie.

Now go about your day. Get some of your Christmas done.

I love you,

ABBA Father

GO MY WAY AND YOU SHALL PROSPER

DECEMBER 9, 2024

I AM about to make your dreams and your pocketbook come true. It is going to be a glorious time for you and your family, MY Precious Children. You have been hoping and praying for so long and the time is upon you.

Everything changes now and it will change in an instant. You say, the economy takes time, and all of this must happen to make it happen for me. Don't doubt Thomas as I AM the Great, I AM and there is nothing that I cannot do.

Stop focusing on the when and look at today. Today is the only day promised. There is no promise of tomorrow. So focus on today and keep your thoughts pure and just and noble and of good report. Think on these things.

Lean not unto your very own understanding but trust in ME as I AM the Great I AM.

Do you know where your sword is? Your sword is MY Love Book. Can you use your sword when needed on a whim? Do you know MY Bible? Have you read it? How do you handle situations? What type of sword do you draw when things go south? Do you use your tongue as a violent sword or do you use MY Word – your greatest weapon in MY Arsenal. Speak MY Word over your situations, in response to others and over yourself and your family. Say MY Beautiful Scripture out loud and pray them back to ME. Dust off your sword and use it. Learn about MY Bible – the love that I have to you and about MY Precious Son, Jesus. MY Love Book is about Him from beginning to end and it is the guide for your whole life. I have given you all of the information to help you to live your best life and the way that I desire you to live. MY Ways are not the ways of man. Many of MY Ways seem backward to the ways of man. Go MY Way and you shall prosper, you and your house.

Now that's enough for today. You have your marching orders.

I love you,

ABBA Father

HELENE VICTIMS, TRUMP & THE EVIL ONES

DECEMBER 10, 2024

Everything will settle down in the government and the world very soon. You are already seeing world leaders showing respect to President Trump. Trump is making the rounds, and you will notice that the Global Elites demonstrate great respect for the US now that Trump is back!

So what to do about the evil ones? Trump is a master chess player, and he did write "The Art of the Deal". Wait and see how he handles them. It will all play out and you will be pleased with President Trump and his administration.

Do you have your shopping done for Christmas? Have you given something for MY Son? Give with no expectation of a gift in return. Give with no expectation of even a thank you. Give your best whether it be a physical gift, money, time or something else. Look at the talents that I have given you. If you can bake, bake something for someone or sew something for someone.

Use what you have and can and give to others. Look for places to sow into MY Kingdom.

What do you think about the mountains in North Carolina? People are dying and no one is saying a word. They think no one is noticing; but they seem to have forgotten about ME. I AM noticing and these precious children that are freezing to death in tents are with ME. For those who orchestrated Helene for greed, gain, power and money – turn from your wicked ways. For those in the US Government ignoring North Carolina and all of the Helene victims, you need to turn from your wicked ways and before it is too late, and you meet ME face-to-face. Repent and turn before it is too late.

Look and enjoy the Christmas season. Sit and reflect on the reason for this beautiful time of year when you celebrate MY Son's birth. Remember I love you with all of MY Heart.

~Adonai

ZELENSKY, THE DEEP STATE & TRUMP

DECEMBER 13, 2024

You have much to be thankful and grateful for this Christmas season. You have been through the toughest of days and Glory Days are upon you. Look up and start praising ME, the Great I AM for the Glory that is starting to fill the earth. You may not can feel it yet but O' you will and very, very soon.

Do not confuse the events happening in the world as coincidence or that it is just time. No, I AM the Great I AM and I AM orchestrating everything for the good of MY Precious Children.

Soon you will no longer see Zelensky from pounding the doors of your Congress for billions of dollars for who knows what. He is not who he seems and the charade is about up.

Trump has told him how it will be and very soon. Zelensky will exit the world stage you see.

Watch moves by Melania and Baron. They are both extremely intelligent and they are both extremely instrumental in the chess moves of Trump and they have his ear.

261

Trump and Team Trump are on the move and are already making great progress for the US to be the fiercest, respected world leader that I created her to be. The snakes that sat in the White House with Trump in Term 1 are gone and have been visibly silent. There has been strife behind closed doors, but now Trump is not to be sidelined by back-stabbing family members and friends he thought he could trust. He understands the Deep State and the Bats that are controlling this deep, dark tangled web of conspiracies to kill, steal and destroy MY United States and her people. No more, I say, no more. The deep state will be cleaned out and the swamp will be drained. I have Trump to drain the swamp and drain he will. Trump will focus on the economy and the border while the cabinet drains the swamp. Wait and see! There are bold, brave men and women that Trump has picked and aligned himself with. This team will be fiercely loyal unlike the Term 1 team.

And so Happy Christmas and a Happy New Year (John Lennon playing in my head). 25' will be the greatest year for the US. The news will beam with victory after victory for Team Trump. The economy will be great, and your purse will be heavy. Remember to thank ME as you move from glory to glory. I AM moving in your life, and you will prosper and be free in the days to come.

MY Children who have been attacked by witchcraft – speak against this evil. Rebuke and bind it and command it to leave your life in MY Son's name, Jesus. Spend time with US to heal what has happened in your life. You trusted that one and knew not their dark side. I AM setting you free. Whom the Son sets free is free indeed. Now praise ME and MY Son for your freedom and forgive that one for their evil they sent against you. Your part in this is forgiven as far as the east is from the west. Now rest in your freedom and praise MY Son Jesus for paying the ultimate price for you to be free. Halleluia! Amen! Amen!

Are you celebrating MY Son's birthday? You say, I have no one to celebrate with. The family is jacked up and everyone is gone. No, you celebrate, and WE will celebrate with you. Find a way to give a gift even if it is to volunteer somewhere or money to help others and to spread the Gospel of MY Son. Don't miss MY Son's birthday even if you are alone. WE are with you. Honor Him the King of Kings with your praise and thanksgiving. It's Christmas! Be grateful and of good cheer!

We love you with an everlasting heart.

~Adonai

DIDDY, EPSTEIN, DREAM AND MY REMNANT

DECEMBER 14, 2024

It is time for you to see the wonder and the splendor of all I AM going to do in your life and those around you. You have not because you ask not. Dream big and bigger and as you dream write it down in a journal and then ask ME for the desires of your heart.

I AM the Great I AM and there is no one like ME. Nothing is impossible with ME. Now dream, ask and believe.

There is much going on in the world. Much looks bad and quite evil, but I AM moving and shaking this earth and soon you will see much revealed, exposed and coming to the surface of all that the evil ones have done. Much will amaze and disgust you. The Diddy's and the Epstein's are coming out. The treasonous acts are coming out and soon you will see and know who all of these people really are. Their shame and humiliation will not begin to take care of what they have done. Biden is working hard to pardon as many as will pad his wallet. But Kash and team will figure out where the loopholes are. The prisons will be fuller and for many they will have a room in Gitmo. They will be gone and forgotten except the evil that they caused and how it affected you, MY Precious Children.

Do you even think about the sacrifice that MY Son made for you? The work, agony, pain and torture He suffered to deliver you for all of your sin. To give you a hope, peace, joy and love. To give you a future and for all of MY Goodness to pour on you. MY Son is Love and He volunteered for the mission HE took for you. WE would not have had it any other way. WE needed a perfect without sin or blemish sacrifice to atone for the sins of the world and MY Son freely did it all for you. WE love you so much. Choose Him today and start truly living. Choose Him today and begin your greatest life now. Jesus said there would be tribulation and there will be until the end of the age but fear not MY Little Ones as WE will never leave you nor forsake you. The days of tribulation - WE will see you through and take you from Glory to Glory. MY Promises are true. Amen. Amen.

Now play with your kids. Let them frolic and play. Give them the love and comfort and protect them. Teach them of MY Son and HE will direct their pathways. I gave you your children and I love them so.

Shield your young ones from the evil exposure that is coming. It is the time for MY Glory to pour out on the earth and the multi-billion soul harvest.

I AM raising up MY Remnant and soon you will know them. I kept them hidden for many years. MY Remnant have been faithful in their pursuit of ME and MY Son and

I AM going to reward them greatly. Much of the remnant have privately pursued US and seem like ordinary people. But MY Precious Holy Spirit is anointing each of them with new and beautiful anointings. Remnant, I AM calling you to your post and use the gifts, talents and anointings that WE have put into you.

So, this is Christmas! Find the joy – enjoy the shopping, the wrapping of the gifts and the celebration of MY Son Yeshua's birth. He is the first of many gifts that WE have for you.

Love,

Adonai

109 MANY IN GOV'T & ENTERTAINMENT

SOLD OUT TO THE ENEMY: KATY

DECEMBER 16, 2024

To experience more of MY Goodness, come bask in MY Presence. Come, give ME a few minutes of your day and sit and be still and let ME fill you fresh. Let ME fill you full of US. ME and Jesus and the Precious Holy Spirit. Just spend a few and WE will make all things new. Let US help you on your way each day. WE love you so very much and long for your presence and desire for you to long for OUR Presence. Come.

There is always room at the table for one more. Think of who you can include this Christmas. Is there people you know who will be alone? Ask them. They will not mess up your perfect family Christmas. I have told you in MY Word to be hospitable. Always have an open hand, an open heart and welcome people into your home and holiday celebrations. The love you show to someone else is MY Love through you. Be the Light of MY Son and let others see MY Precious Son through you.

Don't let your lamps grow dim in these days. The enemy is roaming around looking for whom he can devour. He knows his time is getting shorter and he wants to destroy all that he can. Pray for those who have sold out to him that they will repent and receive MY Son Jesus before it is too late for them. There is only one sin I cannot forgive and that is blasphemy of MY Precious Holy Spirit. For those who have not blasphemed MY Holy Spirit, forgiveness is available if they will just reach out and repent. Pray for them. There are many who sold out for fame and fortune. You know them by name. Pray for them and the evil ones in the governments around the world and the US. Many in government and entertainment sold out to the enemy. I still love them and will receive them with open arms if only they will truly repent with a pure heart (visibly seeking Jesus with open arms). Katy, I AM calling you home – return to ME. I love you and you were raised and taught the truth. Jesus is the Way, the Truth and the Life.

Now what do you want to know today? Something personal, global or when MY Son is coming? Give ME your time and I will answer your questions. I will not give you the exact on Jesus' return as WE cannot alert the enemy. MY Son is anxious to come, receive His Bride and to bring you home. Home where there will be no weeping or sorrow. Home to US where you will have perfect peace and a life that you can barely imagine. Home to feel MY Love even stronger. Seek MY Son Jesus now and you will receive this glorious home for all eternity.

MY Prophets are speaking and telling MY Truth, and you listen to them with an attentive ear; but, come to ME, MY Child and let ME speak directly to you. I have secrets and mysteries that I want to reveal to only you. Be still and know ME. I AM not a man that would lie. MY Sheep hear MY Voice, and they know MY Voice.

Now go wrap some presents and hang a decoration. Celebrate MY Son's birth. The greatest day of this year. Ignore the media and all of their commercial hype. Turn away from all that and remember Holy is the night - the night MY Son came as a babe as the lowest of the low, yet the King of All Kings. MY Son's love for you is more than you ever ask or think. It is more than enough.

Make today count. Send another Christmas Card. Hug someone else. We love you so much!

~Adonai

DRONES, KAMALA, & BOBBY KENNEDY
DECEMBER 18, 2024

Tell MY People that I love them. Tell MY People to turn from their wicked ways. Tell MY People to search the scriptures and find ME. Tell MY People to quiet themselves and get to know ME – to know that I AM Love and I love everyone with an everlasting heart. I AM merciful and just. I AM quick to forgive, but I must keep MY Word and the wicked ones will be punished. MY Word is very clear. MY Word is a Covenant between ME and MY People. A Love Book that explains Who ME and MY Son are. A guide for your life and a beautiful love story about MY Son from beginning to end.

You ask about the drones over the skies? They are from your government – to invoke fear in the people and they are surveilling various people and locations. They blame the drones on helicopters, planes, planets and drones. Do not let this evilness fool you as they are wreaking havoc as they get ready to go out the door.

Watch Kamala as she is trying to stir up a future campaign following. She failed this time and there will be no next time. I told you she would die and I have killed her politically. She will keep a few stragglers, but, her followers will turn away as new younger and more polished speakers enter stage left in the coming four years. Kamala's political career is dead. Go home Kamala! And repent of all your lies vile and deceitfulness of the American public.

Watch Bobby Kennedy in the days to come. His words are truth and he knows his stuff. He is a man of great wisdom. The Pharma's, lobbyists, and the FDA will fight their good fight; to keep him out; but, I AM the Great I AM and I pick the ones who will lead this great and mighty land – the USA. MY Bobby has suffered much in his life; but his heart is pure, he loves children. His heart's desire is to make a difference in the lives of the American people and stop autism in this country. Embrace MY Bobby and listen to his wisdom. I placed this wisdom of health in MY Bobby to teach you that MY Precious Children would not perish for a lack of knowledge.

Embrace Bobby and be a supporter of all he brings to the table. I purposely aligned him with MY Trump to make America great and healthy again.

Now Christmas is next week. Are you ready yet? If not do a little today. WE have lights and food and celebration in heaven too. Parties and get-together – all for MY Son. He deserves all of the honor and praise. Give Him the Glory and enjoy celebrating His birthday!

WE love you with an everlasting heart.

~Adonai

THE LEFT, THE PRODIGALS & YOUR INVESTMENTS

DECEMBER 19, 2024

Start packing and unwrapping and planning ahead. Ignore the declines in your investments, your foreign's and your metals. All will be well MY Child as I have promised.

Stage left is wreaking havoc as they get ready to exit and are packing. Some fear they will leave in handcuffs and many of them should. Many have committed crimes against the Great United States and against you, My American people. They are working hard uncovering any strips that will hinder Trump. There will be no hinderances (for Trump).

The markets will restore and all of your investments. Just sit tight and wait. The Golden Age that MY Trump calls it is upon you and yes, it will be golden.

Many of you have been faithful in your pursuing of MY Son. He loves you so and loves how you celebrate HIS Birthday. Jesus loves His Birthday just as you love yours. He hopes to hear from you and see you celebrating Him with a pure, joyful heart.

Give a gift to one that does not expect. Sow a gift in a place that loves MY Son. Read the Christmas Story with family and friends and be sure and tell your children of the Savior's Sweet Birth. Find a place by yourself and give US a few. Christmas is a sweet time that WE want to share with you.

No matter the size of your tree or your gifts – it is all a matter of the heart. Love on those who are hard to love. Love on those who feel less and are unsure of themselves. Do not judge. Just love.

Remember to take no offense at this time. Being offended is not of MY Son – take the chastisement, the criticism and the hostility with love. Remember MY Son came and He taught you to love. If you have trouble with offense and sharing this love, come to US and WE will help. WE can change you and your heart.

The bells will be ringing, and the phones will chime. The Prodigals are coming. So get ready. Believe and ask ME one more time. Be prepared for them and open your heart and your home. Some will bring more with them and the reunion will take time. Be patient, MY Love as they are nervous and afraid. They are coming expecting to be treated as outcasts – like MY Son told you in His Parable of the Prodigal Son. So, study that now and be like that father. His son had come home and he honored him and gave him the best. Be like that father and take no offense. Just love on your child and give ME thanks. I AM a good Father. They are not condemned by ME and you don't either. Just love. Now get ready. There are things to do. Presents to wrap and cookies to bake. Make some extra and share with someone new. Gifts open doors and may give you a chance to speak of MY Son's Birth.

So get ready MY Darlings for the day's dawn. Merry Christmas!

I love you so much,

ABBA Father

FINANCES WILL CHANGE IN AN INSTANT!

DECEMBER 20, 2024

So, this is Christmas! And a Happy New Year and yes, it is going to be the grandest, most wonderful year for MY Dear Precious Children. You have wanted, hoped and prayed. You have saved, invested and hoped. Watched the values and the markets and even got mad at the Prophets for events not happening in your time zone. Now is the time. I have great, golden plans for all of MY Children. You have sown into MY Son's Kingdom with faith, hope and belief and I AM going to greatly reward you for what you have done and much, much more. The rewards are for you to enjoy and to continue to sow into MY Son's Gospel for the Great Final Multi-Billion Soul Harvest. I have told you this time and again and I want to remind you as this is the eve of the day you celebrate the birth of MY Most Dear Precious Son Jesus. Another gift I have for you to remind you of what is to come.

There still will be things going on in the world that are not of ME. The enemy will be active; but MY Glory shall fill the earth, and you will see miracles, signs and wonders. A Great Wealth Transference that only I can do. I AM the Great I AM, and I have told you time and again. The wealth of the wicked is laid up for the righteous. For MY Righteous Precious Children, it is time. Finances will change in an instant. Homes and land will be <u>given</u> to many, and many will receive inheritances. Do not fret or worry of how I will do it. I AM the Great I AM, and nothing is impossible with ME. Just wait and see. Be excited and expectant like a new Mom to be. Anticipation and wondering about the unknown. But excited for the future, as you know it is bright and full of wonder.

My Son wants His Bride and WE want you home. So, get ready MY Children for the way Home is glorious. But first, before you come home, WE all have work to do. WE do not want to leave any behind that will be MINE. Get to your posts MY Children and Remnant arise. It is the multi-billion soul harvest. You see it is a three-part mission: MY Glory, the wealth for the harvest and then the harvest comes in. Be a part of the Great Final Harvest. The souls of the people of this earth are on MY Heart and MY Son said the workers are few, but the harvest is ripe and ready. Be a harvester in these final days and help US make heaven crowded. WE love all and want none to perish. WE grieve over the lost as a mother grieves over her lost child. Lay-up treasure in heaven and do not squander the wealth and abundance that is coming into your hands.

So this is Christmas and a very Happy New Year! It is going to be a good one without any fear. I gave these words to John Lennon. Enjoy them and celebrate and love one another. We love you so much more than you can ever ask or think.

Merry Christmas!

ABBA Father

THE SHAKING! IT IS COMING!

DECEMBER 22, 2024

It will come in one night and one day. A 24-hour shaking that will change everything. And I mean everything in one day. The markets will change. Your lifestyle will change, and your family will change.

They think they have you over a barrel and they seem to have forgotten about ME. I AM not a man that I would lie. Because I have not done anything dramatic that has been written about in the Bible in about 2000 years, the naysayers will tell you that I don't move like that anymore. I AM the Great I AM and there is none like ME and there never will be. The shaking is coming, and it will be soon. I must move as the evil ones seem to have no heart or soul left. I told you before I AM waiting on the last one to repent that will. Pray for the evil ones again and again – before it is too late for them.

Your prayers are powerful, and My Son is the Savior. Pray that they will turn from their evil wicked ways. You are seeing evil at it's worst and they will know that I AM not playing quite soon.

Now don't fret or worry MY Precious Child. I know where you are always and will protect you from all harm. When the shaking occurs, all hands must be on

279

deck as there will be causalities and there will be harm; but MY Sweet Children will not lose not even a hair on their head.

Now it is Christmas. 25' will be golden, but for now I want you to spend time with your family and call an old friend. Love on your children and tuck them in bed. Pray for the lost and give a little more.

Expect the best Christmas and even more to come.

I love you with an everlasting heart.

~ABBA Father

DEATH AND DESTRUCTION TO THE EVIL ONES

DECEMBER 26, 2024

The winds of change are upon you. Can you feel it? Can you sense it in the atmosphere? Yes, MY Child change is coming. A change that you have never seen before. A change that the people of MY Eart will welcome. Do not fear what is coming. After the shaking stops, you will be thankful for the shaking. Fear not the shaking. As the Shaking is to cleanse and to give MY Children a message to turn back to ME and MY Precious Son Jesus. Turn back. Turn back. WE love you so much and WE want none to perish.

The winds of change will bring great gifts and prosperity for MY Precious Children. The winds of change will bring death and destruction to the evil ones. All will not die, but there will be death. I have told you the death angel is on the move. And move he will. Be vigilant and prayed up. This does not mean that you have to stop your life or neglect your loved ones to be prayed up. Look at MY Son's Beautiful Prayer to ME. He taught you to pray in a brief amount of time and His Prayer is all powerful and covers all of the bases. There is nothing missing, nothing lacking. Don't misunderstand MY Child, WE love for

281

you to spend time with US. Please stay a little longer and talk and commune with US all day. But prayers of faith that are powerful and effective do not have to be long and drawn out. Pray like MY Son. Pray to ME, ask and just simply believe.

Believe you have what you said. Believe it is done and stand. Long prayers are wonderful as it gives US more time together; but, I want you to believe at the moment you pray at the beginning. Faith moves MY Heart and is the currency in heaven to get your prayers answered. I love your prayers MY Child. Please don't make them fancy. Be yourself that I created with ME and MY Son. WE love simply you. Not some pretend part of you.

For MY Loves who feel less than or have allowed yourself to become someone that you think I cannot love, stop! I love the way you are. I love you when you are wayward, when you are in sin. I love you. Come to ME and let ME guide you back on the beautiful path of life that I have for you. Come to MY Son. Invite Him into your heart and repent of your sin. Come to US and WE will change your life, your heart and you will never regret bending your knee to MY Son, Yeshua, the King of Kings and the Lord of Lords. Come. The invitation is open, and the door will one day close. You know not when. So, choose wisely now MY Child as this is a forever decision.

The year 25' will be the best year to be alive. O' there will be drama in the governments and on the streets. But happy, glorious days are upon you, and all of MY Precious Children. Let US in and fill your life with OUR Love that surpasses all understanding. Let US give you the peace and prosperity that you long and desire for. Come give US a few minutes of each day. I never ask you for hours and hours. Just a small amount of time. You have work to do and people to care for.

So, go now MY Child and do your tasks and love on those people that I have put in your paths. Let them see ME and MY Son through you. I love you so much through and through.

~ABBA Father

2025 – THE BEST YEAR TO BE ALIVE!
DECEMBER 28, 2024

2025 will be the best year to be alive. The Glory is coming and come it will Trump will take office and the economy will rebound. Your purse will get heavy and your bank account(s) too

Many of you will need new bank accounts and investing will increase. You will see returns like never before and you will cheer and rejoice; but remember to praise ME more.

Trump will lower taxes, and you will be amazed as taxes continue to go away. The tariffs imposed will fix the nation's deficit problem and soon Trump will announce that the USA no longer has a debt, and we are a debt free nation.

As the nation's debt decreases, yours will as well. Many of you will see Nesara and overnight debt cancellation. This financial freedom will come in many ways, and I have created the best for each one of MY Precious Children. Don't worry or fret how your financial freedom will come but come it will. I have the best plan for each of you and it is tailor made just like you

The wars will cease. Wait and see. The move's being made now with ensure the steps that will take care of the wars

Israel will be free and deal with Hamas. No more attacks on MY Beloved Israel ~the apple of MY Eye. Come January 20th Russia will settle down. They are causing a stir as they know they can with a spineless puppet government alive in the US. But January 20th will come, and Day 1 will start the peace you have hoped for and longed for throughout MY World

I am using Trump and the USA and the players coming in place to set you free from all of this evil tyranny.

The arrests will be made, and the evil will be gone. I have promised you My Dear Ones. They will be gone

Watch the skies in the days to come. There will be signs in the heavens and all over the air space. Night flights are carrying out their missions and these are from ME. I give men the direction and the ideas they implement

The border will close, and the country will expand. Watch Trudeau and Greenland and see what I do next.

The world will respect the USA again and the peace will last when MY Glory is here. I have told you seven years of Glory and seven it shall be. Remember seven years of plenty in Egypt and then the drought. It is a sign of what is to come. The Harvest, The Glory and the plenty and the overflow.

The Remnant will rise and rise they shall. You are meeting them now. They are MY Beloveds who have paid a great price, and I AM raising them up as a reward and an honor. Shelly and Ash and many like them will do great and mighty things in MY Kingdom and on MY Behalf.

You will soon see the Multi-Billion Soul Harvest and be a part of this now. Don't delay to get on with working the fields. The harvest is great, and the workers are few. WE need all hands-on deck. All of you. Tell all of your friends near and wide of MY Precious Son Jesus and the Love for His Bride.

My Son wants His Bride home, but it is not quite time. Would you want to leave some others behind? So, WE wait on those who will choose MY Son. WE give all every chance and will not close the door until WE know their decision for MY Son or to choose the evil one.

So, prepare for 25' the best year to be alive. You will sing and dance and watch the world change. It is a new dawn of an era of Glory. Trump calls it Golden, and I call it Glory.

You were created and made for such a time as this. The hard days are about over, and you will be rejoicing. Stay close to ME and look to the East. MY Son is returning, and I AM getting it all in place. I AM a good Father, and I do not lie. Trust ME and thank ME.

I love you so much,

ABBA Father

THE MUSIC INDUSTRY WILL CHANGE – BEYONCE, MADONNA, RHIANNA, TAYLOR & KATY & OPRAH TOO!

DECEMBER 31, 2024

MY Angel Armies are on the move. It is 2025 and it is the greatest year to be alive. You are going to be so amazed at what I do in the earth this year and the next seven. Everything changes now. The morning has dawned, and it is time for MY People to rejoice.

Rejoice that I AM saving you from the evil ones. Rejoice that your prosperity is right on top of you. Rejoice your loved ones are saved and living for ME. Rejoice your family is restored. Rejoice you have peace in your home and in the streets. Rejoice the rogue government is in custody and the evil ones are gone. Rejoice the wars and rumors of wars are fading away and now is the time for peace throughout MY Land. Rejoice for MY Glory and the multi-billion soul harvest. Rejoice that it is well with you. No more sorrow, sickness, pain and disease. No more debt, lack and no more creditors calling. Rejoice as these promises I made, and you will see and taste all of this in the year 2025.

Rejoice the evil is being exposed and I AM a merciful Father, but I AM just and the evil ones must pay the penalty for high treason and crimes against humanity. And pay they will. Many with their life. But for some of those, this is what it will take for them to finally turn from their evil ways and choose ME and My Son, Yeshua. Many will not humble themselves and their fate is sealed for all eternity. But I AM just.

This grieves ME as it grieves you to punish your child, but choices are made, and they know the consequences. Pray for the evil ones again. Your prayers are powerful, and WE are moving in the hearts of the few that will bend the knee and repent to ME and MY Son Jesus. WE love them so and want them all to repent. But many will not. Pride, arrogance, selfish ambition, lust and greed are many of the sins they have branded themselves with.

You have watched much of Hollywood empty out as many are leaving this deep, dark place and choosing a better, brighter life for themselves and their children.

The music industry will soon be turned around as their evil, satanic messaging in their shows will be stopped. The symbolism and hand signals are not of ME. They are of the enemy. The color coordination is to lure you in. Do not be deceived and teach your children well. Their shows of worship to the evil one will stop and come to a halt and I will deplete their bank accounts, take their lavish home and the clothes on their backs. How dare they try to deceive and lure MY Young Ones into the occult and worship of the evil one? They are not going to be remembered for the beauty and gifts that I gave them, but their fatal fall that takes it all. (They are on a slippery slope). I AM done with them and MY Music shall be beautiful and meaningful and give peace and joy to MY People. Enough of their shows that depict hell and the evil. Turn them off and shield your children. Watch them fall and pray for them.

They went to the dark side to advance their career and have this grand lifestyle that does not fulfill. They may be rich in the world's eyes, but for most of them, their life is shallow and empty and they are poorer than MY Poor Ones. Pray for them and especially Katy. She is always on MY Heart. I love her so.

Beyonce and Madonna and Rhianna – repent. Your days are numbered and soon it will be too late. You each know better; but you think you know best. Taylor, how dare you lead MY Young Girls down the path of destruction. Fall you all will if you don't choose to repent. Pray for them again before it is too late.

Oprah, there is only one way to ME. Repent and turn before it's too late.

You each have great influence, but you cannot forget ME. You have ignored ME and said I will have time to repent. Do you? Choose wisely today as MY death angel is moving. The doors will close suddenly. What side will you be on?

So, MY Children I give you great news. This year will be wonderful and the best year to be alive. Come close to ME and give ME a few. Look for ME in your everyday life. Be an everyday person – humble and meek. Be bold like MY Son and have great compassion for all. Be the bright light in the ever-present darkness. MY Glory is coming and there is no time to waste. Study and pray and tell people of MY Son. This life is but a vapor and then you will be done. Lay up your treasures in MY Heavenly Vault. When I open your book, your treasures will fall out. Be excited and expectant and this year will be grand. Choose wisely MY Children as the time is at hand. Today, fix your thoughts on ME and MY Son, what is pure and lovely and all that's good. Turn away from all evil on your TV and news. Enjoy MY Creation and the loved ones I have given you.

25' will be glorious – a gift to MY Children. Enjoy this year as the Glory has arrived.

~Amen

Made in the USA
Monee, IL
13 January 2025

3e588c29-7a09-4991-babf-532b480b6dc8R01